Compiled Poems

Compiled Poems

1957–2022

David Davis

Copyright © 2024 by David Davis

All rights reserved. No part of this book may be reproduced or transmitted in any form or by any means, electronic or mechanical, including photocopying, recording, or any information storage and retrieval system, without permission in writing from the author.

ISBN: 978-1-6653-0718-5 - Paperback
ISBN: 978-1-6653-0719-2 - Hardcover
eISBN: 978-1-6653-0720-8 - eBook

These ISBNs are the property of BookLogix for the express purpose of sales and distribution of this title. The content of this book is the property of the copyright holder only. BookLogix does not hold any ownership of the content of this book and is not liable in any way for the materials contained within. The views and opinions expressed in this book are the property of the Author/Copyright holder, and do not necessarily reflect those of BookLogix.

Library of Congress Control Number: 2024900490

∞This paper meets the requirements of ANSI/NISO Z39.48-1992 (Permanence of Paper)

011524

For Kathy and Elizabeth, with hope they understand.

Introduction

These poems are in very roughly chronological order. I have grouped them by where I lived when I wrote them, as best as I can remember, but they are not in order of composition. The earliest I wrote was in elementary school, the latest after I retired from CDC, so the timespan is noticeable. Some are massively bad; others might be worthwhile. I hope there is some improvement over the years. Some are autobiographical, most just have autobiographical elements but do not tell the whole truth, and some have nothing to do with me whatsoever. But I guess this is as close to an autobiography as I get.

Virginia Verses (pre-1964)

One Little White Butterfly

One little white butterfly
Fluttering, fluttering by
Tell me who, who is my love
Tell me who, who is my love
Two little whiter butterflies
Fluttering, fluttering by
Tell me who, who is my love
Tell me who, who is my love.

Jenny Jones

Jenny Jones don't look at me
Jenny Jones don't stare at me
That's not polite you see
Jenny Jones don't look at me
Jenny Jones don't stare at me
I've been working hard and now I'm tired
Jenny Jones don't look at me
Jenny Jones don't stare at me
That's just the way it has to be
Jenny Jones don't look at me
Jenny Jones don't stare at me
I'm just one of those kind
Jenny Jones don't look at me
Jenny Jones don't stare at me
Someday I'll make something of myself
And then you'll see
Jenny Jones don't look at me
Jenny Jones don't stare at me
Jenny Jones
Jenny Jones
Jenny Jones.

Fairforest Beginnings (1964–66)

The Spirit That Haunts the Halls Of Fairforest

There is a spirit that haunts the
    halls of Fairforest;
An elusive spirit that haunts
    the halls of Fairforest
Sometimes he is there and never noticed,
    the spirit that haunts the halls of Fairforest
Sometimes he is not there and he is missed,
    the spirit that haunts the halls of Fairforest
We must join together to find and keep
    the spirit that haunts the halls of Fairforest
He is needed and wanted
    the spirit that haunts the halls of Fairforest
We have him and yet we do not
    the spirit that haunts the halls of Fairforest
He is school spirit
    the spirit that haunts the halls of Fairforest.

Three Haiku

Soldiers they do die
But don't know the reason why
But their children do.

I cannot love
That I know but don't know why
But yet I desire it.

I want to know all
But I know I can't, only God
Can, but I try to.

Black and Blue

Black and Blue
I should be black and blue
Black and blue
I should be, I should be
Black and blue
Since you left me
Since you hurt me
I should be black and blue
But I am only blue for you.

Great Scott

Great Scott in the dawning
That's what I said
Great Scott in the dawning
As I jump out of bed
Great Scott in the dawning
Don't me imped
Great Scott in the dawning
The sun is red.

Yuma Yearnings (1966–69)

Who Am I?

Who am I? Do I know?
Perhaps, at least a little bit
Does anyone else know me?
No.

Proverb

A penny saved is one less piece of bubble gum.

Halloween Night

I'm walking down the street you see
I turn the corner and oh my oh me
A ghoulish, horrible face I see
Oops, sorry Mary, I didn't recognize you
without your mask.

Christmas

Christmas, when the babe was born
lying in the hay
Christmas, when new ties are worn
always bright and gay
Christmas, when one should sleep
but is up at break of day
Christmas, when you smile and say
it is a delightful day.

Kofa in the Morning

Kofa in the morning at first is quiet
with only the sound of the wind and the birds
       and your own lonely footfalls
Then the silence is shattered as the Byrds
       begin to sing along with the birds
Hundreds of feet clatter and clack
Hundreds of voices talk of nothing and the world
In this place of learning a new day
       of experience begins
The day will soon be forgotten, but what is gained
       during it is not so soon left behind.

She Was a Pathetic Sight

She was a pathetic sight
She looked like a very skinny Tiggy
       who needed dental work
Her eyes somehow didn't seem to be working together
But maybe that was just the effect of the six-inch bangs
Which, unfortunately, did not cover her six-inch ears
I looked down and saw that her feet were ever so
       slightly bigger than mine
The dress covered her knees, but one could every so often
       hear the faint tap of bone on bone
I looked at her and she smiled
       shyly, understandingly
And I said
       I do.

Go Away Man

Go away man
Go far away
And leave me to my mountain
Go away man
Go far away
And leave me to my hill
Go away man
And leave me to my trees and breezes and skies and clouds
Go away man
And take your manners and rules and social pressure
Leave me to dress the way I like and talk the way I like and act the
      way I like
Take your hints and tact and little white lies
And leave me the cold hard truth
Take your world and your women and your whole society
And leave me to make my own
For I am what I am
And I can be nothing more
And what I am is between me and my God
Not between you and the world
Go away man
And leave me to my songs and laughing children and gentle breezes
Go away man
Take your fights and hates and dreams and beautiful tomorrow
Go away man
And leave me to my mountain.

Tear Drops

Diamonds of sorrow they are
Sparking with sorrow they are
When one cries
A little part of him dies.

The Sea

Rolling in and out
Moving all about
Carrying us about
Once in a while a pout
Acting like a lout
But standing oh so stout.

How People Get an Education

The rich buy it with money
The poor with good, hard work
I buy mine with blood, sweat, and tears
How do you buy yours?

Desert Rain

It is hot
The sun beats down on the dead brown desert
Far away over the mountains a hit of vapor
And soon the rain of spring
The desert flows silver
And the cloud goes
And man goes
And life goes
All that is left is the sun and the dead brown desert
And a flower blooms.

The Miracle Cure

I got a sore back a few days ago
Went to a doctor man I know
He said man, you got an infection
Here's some medicine, follow directions
Medicine made me sick
Feet swole up and my back still itch
Doc sent me to another man
He gave me more medicine, told me to lie outside in the sand
Now my back still itch and my feet still sore
And I got a rash and even more
The thought of going back makes me shudder
Why, I might wind up six feet under.

When No One Cares

The loneliest man in the world am I
Because I never need to say good-bye.

Do You Know Yourself?

Man all through life will hear his voice
    and see his mirror image
But very few will look and know
    exactly where his heart is.

Come, Follow Me

Come, follow me
There are two roads
Down that road there are lights and
      cities and great things
Down my road there is a flower
Come, follow me
Down that road there are gold and
      money and riches
Down my road the sun is shinning
Come, follow me
Down that road are fame and
      glory and greatness
Down my road is a child laughing
Come, follow me.

Who Am I?

Who am I?
Doesn't anyone know or care?
And the answer comes back from out of the air
No!
They just smile; go on their way
don't listen to what you say
They don't care who you are
or which star is your star
For if you dream a dream
to them it just must seem
to be a thing which cannot be
For lonely though you are
stay pointed toward your star
Forget man and those sinking things
Just let your mind reach out
And then without a doubt
You'll find just who you are.

Footsteps Knocking on the Floor

Footsteps knocking on the floor
But no one's knocking on the door
All this says is no one cares
No one's longing to see me
Footsteps knocking on the floor
Only tell me no one's knocking on my door
Maybe someday you will see
That I can be only me
And footsteps knocking on the floor
Will change to knocking on the door
Then will be just you and me.

My Heart Is Weary

My heart is weary
My soul is tired
I wish I could find a rest
But I know I'm working
      for God's own cause
And I know He never rests
My mind is sick of people
      and sin
I wish I could go away
But from within comes my dear Lord's cry
You must carry on for awhile
So I struggle and strive
      till my soul is sore
And my heart cries out for rest
And from within comes my dear Lord's cry
You must strive just a little more
Just a little more for Jesus
Just a little more for my God
Just a little more then I'll reach the shore
And my heart will find its rest.

Wind Blow My Cares Away

Wind blow my cares away
Wind blow my tears away
Wind blow my tears away
Wind blow my cares away
When that wind she come along
She'll be blowing, blowing strong
I'll pick up and go along
That's why I'm windblown
Wind blow my cares away
Wind blow my tears away
Wind blow my tears away
Wind blow my cares away
When that wind she come along
I'll pick up and go along
Where she's bound well I don't know
But that's where I'm going to
Wind blow my cares away
Wind blow my tears away
Wind blow my tears away
Wind blow my cares away
That's why I'm windblown.

P. J. O.

My dreams fly up on horses' wings
I cannot tell a lie
But I'll keep my blasted mouth shut
Until the day I die.

Last Night I Went to a Party

Last night I went to a party
Boy was I having fun
Cracked a few jokes, told a few stories
And then it all begun
Where did everybody go
Why did everybody leave me
Where did everybody go
Why am I so all alone
Now the jokes weren't bad or dirty
And the stories weren't long or dull
But now I stand in my loneliness
And wonder
Where did everybody go
Why did everybody leave me
Where did everybody go
Why am I so all alone
Why am I so all alone?

Peggy Jean Olin

She had three round scars on her forehead
Just above them her hair was swept back
Only to fall and gently caress her soft shoulders
Her mouth and nose could only be described as dainty
Simply for lack of a better word in the English language
She wore dark, thick glasses
Which only enhanced her already enchanting eyes
She looked like a smooth, polished statue
Made by some master artist of old
Except that she was alive, very much alive
I do not know how this masterpiece came alive
But I do know I would have liked to have shaken that master's hand
For what he made was beautiful.

To an Unknown Girl Who Would Never Understand

It's high time for leaving
Look at the sky
It's high time for leaving
For saying good-bye
I didn't want to leave you
I didn't want to make you cry
But I know I can't stay here
I know the reason why
I've got to keep moving
I've got to wander on
It's high time for leaving
Look at the sky
It's high time for leaving
For saying good-bye
I've got to keep moving
If I'm ever to be free
I've got to keep moving
If I'm ever to be me
I don't want to hurt you
But I've got to go away
I know I'm a drifter
I know I'm made that way
I've got to be lonely
If you love me let me be
For it's high time for leaving
Look at the sky
It's high time for leaving
For saying good-bye.

When My Uncle Died

Mourn him, say your prayers
He is a lost loved one
He is gone, you can do nothing
He has his Heaven, or his Hell
Don't try to remember now
It would only hurt
But if you must do something
Think on his sons.

When It Hurts

A man can feel only so much
After that even the poet falters
I know.

How?

How can I say what I do not know?
How can I express what I cannot feel?
How can I say I love you
When my heart is but a stone.

The Other Road is Worse

To save myself from myself
I have become but a machine
Oh, I long to love, to feel
      to laugh, to cry
But all a machine can know are facts
And facts are lonely things.

Rain

Rain, rain
Keep on coming
Rain, rain
Keep on drumming
You're rolling my cares down the road.

Road of Rainbows

My heart lies in broken scattered pieces
Like burned and broken cobblestone
I feel like a street destroyed
Not because the weight of travelers broke it
But because no one ever ventured there.

Friend

There is loneliness in man
That none can ever feel
Until he knows he has no friend
Another heart can't steal.

I Have a Dream

A dreary night
A dreary day
A dreary heart
A dreary way
A way of loneliness unbroken
A way of greatness yet unspoken
This is my night, my day
My heart, my way.

What's It Like?

What's it like to be a Jew?
I've never been one.
I don't think I ever will be
What's it like to know
    your grandfather died at Auschwitz?
What's it like to know
    you've been hated for centuries
        because you are God's chosen people?
What's it like to know
    you'll always be the different one?
What's it like to be a Negro?
With black skin and a broad nose
And hair that curls forever
What's it like to be
the grandson of a slave?
What's it like to be
the guy everybody looks down on?
What's it like
to have "dirty" skin?
What's it like to be an Indian?
The noble red man
Ignorant savage
What's it like to know
    you once owned all this land
    and roamed free throughout?
What's it like to
    always lose in the movies?
What's it like to
    sell souvenirs and pose for pictures?

I want to know
What it's like to be
    the kind of guy everybody says
    you couldn't understand
    unless you were one?

Meet Me Down

Meet me down where Cherry Lane meets the freeway
Meet me down where we used to hear a lark
Meet me down where there used to be some green grass
Meet me down where there used to be a park
Meet me down where Cherry Lane meets the freeway
Meet me down where tall trees used to grow
Meet me down where we used to hear kids playing
Meet me down where there used to be a park
Meet me down where all you see is pavement
Meet me down where all you hear are cars
Meet me down where three kids died last Tuesday
Meet me down where there used to be a park
Meet me down, I'll have my car, I'll be waiting
Meet me down there, we will drive away
Past the place where Cherry Lane meets the freeway
Past the place where there used to be a park.

Sun Shine High

Sun shine high
Sun shine low
Sunshine where I want to go
I know you
You know me
And the sun shine.

One Sentence Poems

Every year hundreds of people die
of not living.

Jesus has been canceled
        due to lack of interest.

God isn't dead
        he's hiding for shame.

Of course the Holy Ghost is here,
        it's just that no one believes in ghosts anymore.

What if Satan had first and goal to go on the one-foot line
        and you were God's defensive tackle?

If tomorrow is ever to be more than today
        we must remember yesterday.

If I smile at the tears of yesterday
        will I cry over the smiles of tomorrow?

Today is the only thing we ever truly possess
        and we have it only for an instant.

Be what it may
        today is only a day.

Yesterday

Yesterday is a tear
Tomorrow a smile
Today?
Today we go another mile.

Whose Fault?

New semester! Hurrah! Hurrah
Now to get up and run away
From all the classes I'm failing now
Because my teachers don't know how
      to cope with me.

Proverbs

He who laughs last must go see the principal.

Tomorrow, whether it be tear or smile, is precious
If for no other reason, because we have not ruined it yet.

Today, tomorrow is a dream
When I wake up it will be a reality.

Some people live in the past
Some live for today
I live in
   for
   and because of
Tomorrow.

Double Take

I got my pictures back today
Turned them back in right away
The worst thing that could possibly happen
      happened you see
The pictures looked exactly like me.

To Know All

To know all, I desire
But I know that is beyond reach
Still I must strive.

Ode to an Unknown Lover

He sits and stares, but she doesn't see
Everyone dares, but not he
His stony heart a cover
The lonely hearted lover
Sits and dreams of what can never be
For in risking to discover
The lonely hearted lover
Found the dream to be sweeter than thee.

A Poem That Came to Me in the Night

The ocean is a heart-span
My eyes are far away
And up upon the mountain
I stop and bow to pray.

The Freest Man

The freest man in the world
The loneliest man in the world
Same guy.

My Feet Itch

My feet itch
A mountain calls
I hear the sea roar
Today is gone
Come tomorrow, come
For I am lonely with success
And must travel on.

I Am Empty

I am empty
The stone wall built around nothing
I cannot feel
I have no emotions
I cannot cry
I know what it is to love because I cannot
I know what joy is because I cannot feel it
I know what fear is because I cannot be afraid
I know and feel all things more than any man
      because I know and feel nothing
I am empty
The stone wall built around nothing
For when there is nothing, nothing can venture past
      except it be noticed.

Lonely Silence

Lonely silence
A long still walk
In an empty place
Behold God
Know thyself
There is little enough beauty left to us
That we should try to create more
Before we recognize what we have
Walk lonely with me
To a silent, empty place
Behold God
Know thyself
See the beauty I see everywhere
And know why I stand
Soft and silent, smiling
Daring to understand.

Get Happy

Get happy
Burst out like a flower
This can't last forever
Spring only comes four times a year.

Gentle Me Down

Gentle me down by the river
Gentle me down by the stream
Gentle me down ere I love you
Gentle me down or so it seems.

Spring Is

Spring is
      A robin lighting on my shoulder
      A lily not quite yet in bloom
      A sunrise, a cool wind, and a soft tear for the beauty of it all
      A dress, a girl, a new life just around the corner
      Get up, get out, get going, do something
      Spring is happy.

I Glory in the Sunrise

I glory in the sunrise
I glory in the dew
I glory in the sunset
I glory in you
I glory in the morning
I glory in the sky
I glory in the evening
I glory in your eyes
I glory in your hair
I glory in your sweet, sweet lips
That never have touched mine
I've stared into the sunrise
I've known the morning dew
I've loved the bright red sunset
But I never have kissed you
I've risen in the morning
I've flown into the sky
I've lingered in the evening
But I've never approached you
I've glanced into your deep, deep eyes
But I've never touched your hair
And I've never kissed those sweet, sweet lips
That surround your voice so fair.

To a Girl I Used to Know

To a girl I used to know
Once upon a time
Through a veil of laughter
I cried the tears of love
For many a moon
I played the fool
And loved the part
But now the stage is sinking
And reality comes creeping
As I quote my lines
I feel the terror
For the play is ending
And the love has not yet died.

The World's a Stage

The world's a stage
The setting and the props are fake
All the people are actors quoting lines somebody else wrote
The author's crazy, the director's drunk, and the producer's on vacation
In other words, things are all mixed up
The heroine forgot her part
The hero can't find the door
And if the stage doesn't collapse
I think the audience is going to start throwing tomatoes
And if I weren't so busy laughing
I think I would cry.

Don't You Know?

Don't you know, or am I stupid?
Are you a fool, or are you quiet?
Are you blind, or are you silent?
Should I feel sorry for you
Or do you feel sorry for me?

In the Endless Night Sky

In the endless night sky
I see your face, between the Dipper and the Bear
In my dreams I find you walking
So to sleep I do not dare
The sun does not rise till I see your face
The birds do not sing till I hear your voice
My heart does not beat till I see your smile
I cannot feel until you sigh
And tomorrow the future will claim you
Like the cold claims the butterfly that never knew I was there
I shall continue, but the beauty I knew I must not catch
For fear of giving wound
Is like the memory of that butterfly
It will not fade so soon.

A Girl's Smile

A girl's smile is a masterpiece
Could I have created yours?
Can I take some little credit
For once having made you
Laugh, made you smile
Made you happy for an instant?
If I have made you smile
I have created a masterpiece
Could any man want more?

The Shadows Lengthen

The shadows lengthen in
      the day
And now it's time to go
      away
And when I think of leaving
      you
It's like the feeling of the cold
      cold dew
But I know that I must run
      away
Before my tears they do
      betray.

Lines Left in Question

Lines left in question
To a girl I used to know
As my dreams go flying
The pen dries in glory
But the poem does not end.

Sunshine on the Mountains

Sunshine on the mountains
Through a polka-dot of clouds
Spreads a puzzle pattern
On the ragged earth below
Such is life
Sunshine on the mountain
Sunshine in the vale
Clouds hang o're the valleys
And o'er the tops of hills
And the weary traveler wanders
From dark to light and back again.

There Is a Tribute

There is a tribute to a girl
Whose smile rings out a rhyme
Whose movement is to rhythm
As a woman is to man
But whose mind in gentle pieces
Brings a poet's heart to bow
As this gentle woman wanders
Bringing hearts and minds to glow
Poets cry and try
But they know
Words like she can never flow.

Sing a Song

Sing a song of memories
Pocket full of joy
Maybe we will meet again
No longer girl and boy.

For Want of Nothing

For want of nothing
I desire
To have to know
This is the thing that drives me.

Let the Feeling Come Upon Me

Let the feeling come upon me
Let the words flow fast
Let me know all emotions
Both first and last
Let the rhyme make the rhythm
And the rhythm make the
Reason why I write
For a song with a meaning
Is a delight.

Later on in the Day

Later on in the day
When the stars hang out
And I, asleep, bed-ridden
Search the dream corners of my mind
You come walking, gently floating
When I awake, the smile lingers
The thought lingers, the face lingers
I arise, and in the day you are there
You are as beautiful as the dream
And the dream is as beautiful as you
And which is better I do not know
I do not know.

In a King's Page

In a King's Page
Stone's live
A fig tree blooms
A horse flies
Girls come out of lamps
A miller works in darkness
Wine flows on barges
Double names draw pictures
Longhairs like assassins
One is mulling, mulling, mulling
And I sit quietly smiling
Near a sign that says
Yes, we have no bananas.

First, There Was Lonely

First, there was lonely
Now there are friends
Tomorrow will be lonely again.

Waiting Waits on My Mind

Waiting waits on my mind
As I wait on thine
I must be going faster
Because the time is going slower
And the hour I desire is running away from me
Eternity is long, and the time must come
The minds must meet.

Kofa in the Afternoon

Kofa in the afternoon is hot and dusty
The flowers hunch their backs to the sun
A few students and teachers wander around
Tired of learning and teaching, for a while
The radio fades, coaches shout, maintenance men appear
Only the birds never learn
They just keep on singing.

A Girl I Taught at Bible School

Five of age
And fair of hair
Soft of face
With gentle air
This smiling tornado
With love and care
Drives me slowly to despair.

Many Lines Have Been Written

Many lines have been written
Of loves that could not die
I wrote a few of them myself
But now, suffice it to say
The poem is dead.

Trinity Poems (1969-1974)

The Question

Words without meaning
pound into my brain
as the fear
drives into the loneliness
alone
on my own
I have only myself
Is it enough?
Oh God, is it enough?

My Heart Died

My dear, my heart died a long time ago
I miss it now and then
When I see a person cry
      because he is happy
Or when I see beauty
      a girl, a flower, a poem on a wall
I know the emotion, the feeling
But, like I said, my heart died
      a long time ago
And I miss it now and then.

Is There a Gentle Woman Here

Is there a gentle woman here
A woman who knows
Yet is innocent
A gentle woman
With eyes filled with the depths of peace
A man can find only in
A gentle woman
Is quiet joy
With a soul
One can explore till eternity
A gentle woman
Is found in quiet places
By quiet men
Who search gently
Because they believe
In gentle women
Is there a gentle woman here?

My Teachers Want My Time

My teachers want my time
My mother wants my beard
My roommate wants the TV on till twelve o'clock at night
My father wants some better grades
      so I can get a scholarship
      so he won't have to shell out
      so much cash
My sister just wants me to go away
All I want is knowledge, peace, and God
Don't they see, don't they understand
      aren't they aware?
No, I only fight shadows
      they fight darkness.

Penny Football

Penny football formations
A poor man's solitaire
And I've played so many games
My pennies are rare

Penny football is a lonely game
And I play six-man
My quarterback can't throw too well
But he always seems to win

I guess I wouldn't mind
      losing though
If there was a coach
      for the other team.

Boredom

Boredom boredom boredom boredom boredom
boredom boredom boredom boredom boredom
boredom boredom boredom boredom boredom
boredom boredom boredom boredom boredom.

Silent Song

Hey, sing for us again, Jack
Sing for us once more
Sing for us again, Jack
Like you did before

I once knew a man
Who sang with his hands
He used to teach the deaf to sing that way
And when things were slow
And there was no place to go
We would all relax and simply say

Hey, sing for us again, Jack
Sing for us once more
Sing for us again, Jack
Like you did before

His hands they were so graceful
They told the story plain
I never can forget the way that those hands sang
He taught me his music
Before he went away
And now when I sing, my hands they seem to say

Hey, sing for us again, Jack
Sing for us once more
Sing for us again, Jack
Like you did before
Hey, sing for us again, Jack
Sing for us once more
Sing for us again, Jack
Like you did before

I, Sir

I, sir, am a prophet
Usually of doom
Though I do not choose it so
I choose not my visions
But they are mine
I will do my best with them
I choose not this world
But it is mine
I will do my best with it.

Snarly, gnarly branches

Snarly, gnarly branches
On snarly, gnarly trees
Grow snarly, gnarly skyward
But the leaves they fall on me

The trees grow ever upward
But the leaves grow old and die
The trees look ever upward
But the leaves they block my eye.

Drama Club Party

There's a physics major
In Drama X
Watching from the stage
As the actors display their false façade
      of freedom
And try to act like actors act
      at actors' parties
Creation becomes a falsehood
Behind a built-up image
And I lie when I say that
      I do not play a part myself.

Song 1 (From "They Never Applaud the Poets")

If tomorrow came today, would I notice
If my hair turned white with age
Would I be a wiser man
Than now before you stands
Would I miss the youthful vigor of these days
Would there be a bit more time for playing
Would I be free to speak my mind
Would I be a bit more sure where I'm going
Probably not, but somehow I don't mind

I grew up tall and I grew up fast
I was fifty years old 'fore ten years was past
Looked death in the face from my old sick bed
Learned from him a lesson's never left my head
Walked with a cane when I was twelve
Now I run like the devil but I ain't afraid of hell
Put on my own when I was nine, and I stayed all alone
      till I will be twenty-nine
God, can't you hear me, you're my only friend
My life's in reverse, beginning at the end

As I look back on my old age
I remember all my lessons
But I love these childhood days.

Song 2 (From "They Never Applaud the Poets")

I've known her for about eight years now
My love grows every day
She seems to come alive within me
She expresses what I cannot say
Her smooth, curvy body is beauty
Her voice, the angel's

I rest her on my legs
Fold my arms about her
Caress her with my hands
Lovingly I pour my soul into her
She responds with sounds of ecstasy
We love, my guitar and I.

Song 3 (From "They Never Applaud the Poets")

(With apologies to T. E. Barth)

If all the money I had spent on dreams
now flowed into these arms again
If all the tears I had spent on laughter
now rolled back into my hands
If all the sweat I had spent on beauty
now lay before my eyes
Would it all congeal together
indicating me?

If the sum of what was said about me
echoed in to form a shout
If the sum of what I did for others
now stood a single deed
If the sum of what I ever thought
walked in a lone idea
Would it form my mirror image
or perhaps my twin?

Am I the way I look, or perhaps the way I feel
Am I what you think I am, or am I what I think
Am I everyone who has ever been
or am I simply me?

Song 4 (from "They Never Applaud the Poets")

I . . . love . . . you
Isn't it strange to hear it said
Isn't it strange to ring in your head
Isn't it new, isn't it fine, don't you wish that it was said to you

I love you
You hear it in the movies
You hear it on TV
You hear it from your auntie
But that ain't the same as me
I love you, I love you
I've often tried to say it
But the words just wouldn't come
It's awful hard to say it
When you risk playing the bum

I love you . . . I love you . . .
It's such a well-kept secret
An emotion hid by doubt
But if I never say it
I will always be left out
I love you . . . I love you . . .

Song 5 (From "They Never Applaud the Poets")

Spend a lonely night
In a lonely time of life
Spend a lonely day of a year crying home
Yes this time I'll be gone
When you come to take me home
For I'm gone where I'm bound
Said good-bye to old hometown
Spend a day of a year crying home

Spend a day of a year crying home
Oh good-bye
Spend a day of a year crying home
I'm gone

Spend a day, never more, maybe less, if you're poor
Spend a day of a year crying home.

Song 6 (From "They Never Applaud the Poets")

Just tiptoe to tango
and fake everyone out, ha!
They'll think it's a tango
when you tiptoe about, hey!
People are so easily fooled
they even think this a song, ho!
You can make them think anything
If you just lead them along, hi!

Everyone's a faker, we fake the whole day through
And if we ever do something real
They think we're faking that too
Left foot, Right foot, Hay foot, Straw foot
If you just tell them right
They'll even walk on their nose
      Fake one, fake two, I'm a fake ahead of you, BOOM!

Is this real or is this not?
I don't know, but they're sure not, hum . . .

I think I've just gone over the edge
Just a minute, I'm coming too
Let's make it a threesome, I'm joining you.

Song 7 (From "They Never Applaud the Poets")

She lay softly in the grass
With a book in her lap
Studying biology
Oh, she prays before each meal
Makes a sandwich out of pie
And once in a while she smiles at me

She laughs instead of cries
Lives instead of dies
And feels within her soul
That reason must be wrong if it hurts
She is dew at sunrise
With sugar in her eyes
And once in a while she laughs with me

Guitar on her hips
Dog biscuit in her lips
And a song singing on its own
Just a laugh and a sigh
As she makes the world go by
And once in a while, she's with me.

Love Is a Thing

Love is a thing that dangles from a chain
That everyone sings the praise of
Love is a thing people make movies about
That little children aren't allowed to see
      because they wouldn't understand

Love, sir, is a thing I don't understand
It seems you have to love everybody
      or the SDS will call on you

It seems that if you love your God
> you have to make everybody else love him
> if it kills them

It seems that love is what makes people cry
> if they don't have it
And if they do

People cannot love, sir
They don't know how
And their attempts at love
> end in the down, down, down

If this is love, sir
Perhaps you could show me some hate.

When I Meet

When I meet a girl who is a song
When I meet a poem in female form
This woman will I take to me
And with me she will be
Forever.

Lights Flickering

Lights flickering through a blueish haze
Tell me I've seen better days
As I stand and wait awhile
Maybe time will pass me by

Tomorrow will come a day
Maybe I'll be gone away
Or I may still be here
Hoping for another year

I've got the moving blues
Something got to change, or I'll lose
Maybe someday I'll find my world
Or maybe I'll just find a girl

Lights flickering through a blueish haze
Tell me I've seen better days
As I stand and wait awhile
Maybe time will pass me by.

Moon High, Star Light

Moon high, star light
Burning blue beside the night
Red light, shinning bright
Giving light through the night
Flickering candles in the street
And the girl I wish to meet
All are here, 'cept the last
Good times now are past
Soon the sun will appear
Drive my dreams before its spear
But the night will soon return

It is best I was quick to learn
As I go my merry way
Pray for night and live for day
Oh, if my dreams could live in flight
I wouldn't have to love the night
But the sunlight makes me see
You are you and I am me
In the night we are apart
In the day nothing starts
And so the night is to an end
And the day it doth begin
But my heart it longs to see
You and stars gazing at me.

There Is a Stream

There is a stream that runs through my life
And if the girl of grace who lives by the big stream
Comes to know me
She will give me a great batch
Of that which I desire

For those who read this bit of doggerel
A hidden meaning lies within
Couched in names
And not in hidden sin
For the beloved is a seeker
Who loves to sit by great streams
By the happy one who is there waiting.

Christmas Vacation '69

Blue sky, gray sky
Sunshine through the rain
She has gone now
Left me alone again
How much to fly to New York City
How much to fly away
Christmas is a long time coming
New Year's far away
This much time must pass now
Till my blue sun shine
Next year is a long time coming
When my love is far away
When my love is far away.

Sleep

There is a narrow slit of light
coming from the barely cracked
bathroom door
The glow from the bulb
on the electric blanket control
eeries the room
The heater fan blows soothe
I sink deeper, deeper
reality fading into mists of darkness
The goodness of nonexistence
is glimpsed
My eyelashes become bars
before my eyes
The curtain of blackness
slowly falls
My eyes close.

Bitterness, Sir

Bitterness, sir
Is an all-consuming passion
Mixed with utter frustration
Bitterness is a thing a man gets
And then must rise above
Or it will destroy him
But what causes the bitterness
It's having to fight your ever-loving heart out
For every inch you ever got
All the while expecting
The blow that will throw you back a foot
It's thinking you've risen above all the evil whirling around
And just then the maelstrom drags you down
But worst of all it's trying and trying
Knowing that what you cannot control
Will eventually destroy you
You have no choice but destruction
And I am bitter.

A Memory of Respect

A memory of respect
Floats across my mind
And while it pangs
The emptiness of today
It leaves the sorrow far behind.

To a Girl Who Should be Sitting on a Library Wall Overlooking San Antonio

Black upon black
Form upon form
She sits
Gently
On the stone wall
The night-lit city
A beautiful painting
Destined to fall pale
As her backdrop
Dark pervades
Except for the white city lights
And her white, eye-lit face
My childhood returns
And finds form
In her face
It becomes, somehow
A thing I can understand
And therein lies the beauty
I find
In that silhouette of white.

Freezing

Anne, I am cold
My soul shivers as if I lay in the snow
I wish you lay here beside me
Then you would warm me
I would warm you
We might even melt the snow

But you are far away
Where the snow is real

I would like to lie down and sleep
Till you come
But would I awake?
I must exist till you come
Bringing your warmth
Then I will live again.

A Minor Question

Must my visions be afar ones
That I can never reach
Must my dreams be on the ocean
While I stand on the beach
Must my loves be afar off
Just within my gaze
Must my maze be unending
As one by one I search the ways
Must I spend my life in seeking
Through a blurry haze of pain
Must I always love the sunshine
When I am destined for the rain?

About a Not Too Good Statue of Christ Nailed to the Wall of a Church

That's a heck of a thing to do to a Christ
To wrap him up in rags, give him a bloated belly like a corpse
And hang him from a wall or something
He's even got his head down
Like he lost

That isn't my God, brother
Mine is tough and hard
Used to walking all day
And fighting if the need arose
My God looks you straight in the eye
And hasn't lost a fight yet
      And I'm betting he isn't going to
And the last thing you would be able to do
      Is hang him up on anything
      For more than a few days

That isn't my God, Mac
My God doesn't just hang around
He climbs down and starts the revolution.

Lonely Rider

Lonely rider
Your only friend is the sky
Lonely rider
Watch the world passing by
Lonely rider
You'll have to stop by and by
Lonely rider

The lights seem to shimmer in the dark of the sky
Stars moving faster as I walk on by
Two feet is a lonely pair
As alone I stop and stare at the sky
All by its lonesome a star in the sky
Reminds me of me as I walk on by
When you're all alone, you're the brightest one there
But isn't it lonely way up in the air
Lonely rider
Your only friend is the sky
Lonely rider
Always saying good-bye
Lonely rider
You'll have to stop by and by
Lonely rider.

The Old Man Limps

The old man limps slowly across the field
Now and then an expression of pain
      clouds his chill, red face
Behind him, he leaves the lights and sounds
      of Fiesta
Which, if lonely, at least offered some diversions
      that his lonely room could not possess
He is old, he is lonely, and his arthritic shadow
      follows him slowly into the room
      that offers warmth, if not companionship
He wonders if this is to be his lot in life
      to creep slowly, painfully away
      from life and ever into his own soul
This be the fading of age you say?
      and death will soon be his companion
The old man is nineteen years old
The old man is me.

It's as Cold as Death Outside

A cold day is a morbid thing
It burns my bones
Leaving only dust
The wind blows out candle flames
And leaves me shivering
Fascinated by its cruel beauty.

Fall

People passing by the sad café
No, no it ain't the month of May
As I sit and watch the way
All the leaves are falling down

Wind's blowing from a northern sky
Winter's coming by and by
And the sunshine it is a lie
All the leaves are falling down

Coats and sweaters they appear
Snowing time is almost here
It's about time to be moving on
It's about time to be gone
Good-bye.

The Game

She stood by the rail overlooking the basketball court
The teams were warming up, and the long, high-arched shots
    flew by her face
I, a crowd-hidden figure in the bleachers, stared past the team
    up at her
She looked rather lonely and forlorn just standing there
    above the end of the court
She stayed all through the first half, and whenever the play
    swung to her end of the court, I watched her,
      not the ball
She left at halftime, my attention returned to the game
    and we lost.

My Memories Are like a Campfire

My memories are like a campfire
They warm both heart and soul
They are flint and steel
On a cold, lonely night
They keep me alive and warm
Until another bright sun dawns.

One Day I Watched a Shadow Drift

One day I watched a shadow drift
From left of me to right of this
And while I let the sun head west
Two little birds did build a nest
A cottontail came hopping by
And dared to look me in the eye
I think a flower grew
I know the wind blew
Just enough to wake a tree
Who waved a branch at me
And began to put on a new wig.

Thunderstorm

The sky vibrates
Shaking the leaves from the trees
A flashbulb pops above me
An ocean appears between earth and sky
It overflows
Waterfalls are seen on the cliffside
An inland sea forms at my doorstep
The waves subside
Someone makes a dash for the beach
A god is on my roof, crying
Hundreds of firecrackers explode in the puddles
The ocean has become a stream
The roar of the waves fades with the wind
The sea is gone, and only my wet swimsuit
Remains, to be dried.

We Sat on the Wall

We sat on the wall, my love and I
Thinking we had eliminated each other
It was a November spring
We talked of depression and realism
As warmed by the sun we watched
A pregnant cat lay lazily on the stairs below
She tore her paper teardrop
I tore my kisses before they reached my mouth
I smell winter I said
Have a good day she said
As she walked down to pet the cat
I watched her till she left my sight
Then walked away humming "Yellow Submarine."

Lights That Wink in the Night

Lights that wink in the night
The church on the hill, steeple aglow
Teiane's bar by the road, windows curtained
The My-T-Fine Bar-B-Que, low-lit and empty
The gas station, closed forever
The first bright, then dim lights from the coming cars
High, low, bright, dim
Come on, buddy, dim 'em
And forever the reflectors by the side of the road
That glow only when someone shines their lights on them

I knew a reflector once
Not a bad guy to have around
More dependable than a lamp
But not quite as romantic
Come to think of it, I knew a church once
But she never got out enough
I expect she would have been an old maid
Except an old radical married her
Not much sense, these radicals
I guess he thought he could change her
The bar I knew, she's in LA now
We never really made it
We just didn't fit
I ran one way, she ran another
The bar-b-que is an OK guy
Good to sit around with and talk to
But bar-b-que is going out of style
Only a few left, mostly in the South
Most folks just don't have time for bar-b-que anymore
The gas station is closed too
Just like the one by the road
The new ones, no pop, no candy, no pot-bellied stoves

My kids will never know that old man
And I don't think I could ever explain a pot-bellied stove anyway
The reflector is in the army now
Like I said, a nice guy to have around
But not the kind you invite into the kitchen

As each headlight passes, they seem to grow brighter
Blurring my vision
It makes my eyes water
I know I'm on the right road
To get where I'm going
But I wish that sometime
I could come back by
And stop at the church to pray
Get a little bar-b-que, a little gas
And warm myself by that old stove
And follow the reflectors home
But even as I pass
I know they are gone.

Last Night I Dreamed

Last night I dreamed I kissed a girl
On the cheek
And she smiled
I don't often dream that
Usually, I'm rushing off to save the world
Or something
It's kind of nice just to kiss a girl
And see her happy
It's a lot more satisfying than saving the world
Again.

Wail Ye Banshees

Wail ye banshees
The dead arise
And float overhead
Wail ye banshees
The full moon rises
Call the wolves to the alter
Wail ye banshees
Shadows slide by
Searching for streams of blood
Wail ye banshees
I too walk
My feet echoes on cobblestones
Wail ye banshees
A heart is beating
But the body is dead
Wail ye banshees
Chains flail gravestones
And shackles grip feet
Wail ye banshees
We are treading on graves
And God has turned his head
Wail ye banshees
Bats glimmer starlit
And the sun will not rise
Wail ye banshees
It is coffin time
Someone approaches
Wail ye banshees, wail.

I'd Like to Sit under a Tree

I'd like to sit under a tree
And watch the sun set

And let the grass push me up
And have my eyes twinkle
      in the starlight

But there are people working
And I must do my part
Though, perhaps, if my part
      was staring at starlight
It would be a better world.

The Party

I'm sitting on a wall, drinking a coke, and watching this white cat, see
And a friend of mine comes by and says hi and I say hi
And the sun goes down for no reason in particular
And all these girls are walking by, see
And I'm about full
And the coke can is about empty
And it's about dark
And I think I'll go home and wash my hair
But the cat is still there.

**Epitaph for a Mass Slave Grave Written
by a Southern White over One Hundred Years Later**

Here they lie, Black slaves, now free
Gone where there ain't no segregation
Now they know the truth I learned in youth
That God's a big brown Jew-boy
Praise the Lord and pass the cornbread

Amen, Brother.

Final Fall

A pattern of branches against a blue sky
Are you crying my love
Leaves on the ground going to coal
Are you dying my love

Is it the fall of a child
Who learns to rise
Or an old man
Who rejoins dust

The sky darkens with each breath
The well is yellow with urine
Shouts rend membranes
A prophet is digging a grave

My love is yours, love
Why do I beat you
Can a bruise be a mark of affection
Be this why with axe handle I pound your skull

My brain is polluted now
I run into walls
And shun the door
As too hard to open

The branches are falling this year
How strange, no birds weigh them down
Perhaps the tree is dying
Only one last apple.

A Portrait in Words

A portrait in words
of an emotion in flesh
lies on blank canvas before me
I pace, mixing paint
striving to match my model
I think of gamma rays
screenplays, history's haze
and once in a while of Mona Lisa's smile
Da Vinci, where are you?

A Girl

A canyon behind a blouse
A waterfall over a neck
A guitar walks
        on the most important part of a miniskirt.

Random Notes Made While Walking Around Trinity University at Ten p.m. on May 22nd, a Friday

I'm tired of not loving
I'm tired of saying what people want to hear
Instead of what I mean

There go the lights in the library
There go the lights on the tower
They're turning the whole world out tonight, aren't they

Except the bronze Christ
They're rigging his lights
So he looks like gold

"What the hell are you doing out this time of night?"
"I really don't know."
"OK."

Ah, here comes a fellow with two girls
Doesn't seem fair, does it
Oh well, that isn't my game anyway

I've walked this route before, you know
But friends fade in passing
Voices frighten me now

September is ending
But the month is May

Hand in hand, arm in arm
My stomach growls at their passing

Move on, don't limp

That leg isn't sore
Tonight

The wind is blowing
I'm in the grass now
It's hard to write in the dark

This thing isn't worth a shekel
How the heck do you spell shekel

The wagon is ahead
A memory of freer days

I wonder when they turn the fountain off
It was off at three a.m., last time I was by

They hide lights in the ground now
Up ahead is the one that blinds you when you walk over it

You know, it's surprising how many lighted places there are to write
       around here
I'm going to have to get a new notepad
This one is about empty.

Carolina

There is a beauty here
A Carolina four-lane
Red lights to the fore
White lights a la left
Green Pine singing back-up
For the soft-rock radio
My blood kin live and lie here
I guess I've got as many relatives
As this state has churches
And that's enough to get a man heaven
      or a free meal
Depending on which he wants right then
I'm tied to the worn-out soil
This rough red rope of love
I walk a cemetery, 1804, 1756, 1690
That's a darn long rope
Yeah, sure there's a lot wrong out here
We're kinda poor, a little rough, even backward at times
But look at the trees, walk the hills, eat the food
Lota love and trust out here
      for the man who knows how to keep it
There's a Rebel in a man out here
You can go away for a while
But Johnny Reb, he always comes home.

Of Time and the River

Of time and the river
They roll slowly on
Yes time and the river
They never are gone
I rolled out of Denver
One sunny Sunday

I left the mountains
And my heart that day
I crossed the river
And time yesterday
Now I'm going homeward
In tomorrow to stay
Of time and the river
They roll slowly on
Yes time and the river
They never are gone.

How Shallow a Swath

How shallow a swath
Cut by countless men
That leaves not a trail to follow
He lived and he died
And in between, he existed
We think
There really isn't much to go on
Not even a trace Boone could follow
Yet how strange it is
This trackless path
Unworn through eons and ages
Men still travel
In search of a leader to follow.

Logic

This is a non-rhyming
Nonsense rhyme
Which is nonsense
Of course.

Mana

Canary, my free bird
Your spirit lifts o're your song
Soaring skyward
Making reason dance the Virginia Reel
Every free thing must love you
For you are most free
For all of us poets
God in his mercy
Made thee.

Pamela, Oh Pamela

I remember Pamela
When dawn is in the air
I remember Pamela
And the soft brown of her hair
I remember Pamela
When joyous for a while
I remember Pamela
And her rippling, bubbling smile
But best do I remember Pam
When I'm down and out and low
For the life she gave to everyman
Who sat a while in her glow
Yes, I remember Pamela
A girl the world should have known
Oh, I knew her but a little while
And her memory will not go.

I Haven't Got a Song

I haven't got a song to sing
I haven't got a friend to cling to
I haven't got a rhyme to write tonight
I'm just lonesome walking in the eve
Raindrops falling cry for me
I've done the work I drown myself in
Now I walk, no reason to come in
Now I walk, the same place I have been
I'm just lonesome walking in the eve
Raindrops falling cry for me
They make a rhythm on the ground
In starlight's twinkle rhymes abound
God's creation comes and walks with me.

An Old, Old Song

Oh please come and see
the factory-made trees
round the stadium
of synthetic grass
There's a highway nearby
so there's smog in your eye
and the rumble of Mac
makes you tremble
The plastic green trees
wave not with the breeze
but shake with the rush hour jumble
We watched the zoo die
and the cliffs gently crumble
the stadium fell down on second and ten
and does anybody want to buy
a university
cheap?

The Birthday Present

A music stand that folds and tucks away
But pops back out when I want to play
A surprise, I admit, as love always is
You'd think I would learn after twenty years
A dollar here, a dollar there
Dollars I know they could not spare
So is love expressed
Even on a day when it is legal
To say I love you.

Epistle to Pam

You said, "Write me a passionate love letter"
but I can only write about what I know
I thought I might tell you about lambda equals h over p
but physics and logic ain't your thing, thank goodness
Maybe a poem, I thought, fancy, frilly
and full of poetic tricks
but I am too honest, I fear
Perhaps nothing, let it pass
another word left unspoken
the paradoxical pinnacle of a poet's power
You are loved by many
and I contradict myself
There is another like you, you know
Her name is Mana, and I knew her
but that was when I was old
many years ago
You defy metaphor, I guess you realize
Aristophanes would have killed himself
(Sorry about that, but I'm studying Greek History,
and I just had to throw that in)
What can you say about a nightingale

except Shelly amen
I choose my life, let none question that
Yet, if, being what I am, I love beauty
(an old, dead word, Scott would scold me
yet he too failed to capture you in words)
an adjective alien to humanity
may I not be forgiven if for an instant
or two I leave my snowed-in mountain
for the pot-bellied stove of your company
If by chance you read this, realize
that it matters not if you understand
or not, merely that I have written
I, who cannot love, have written,
in love, to love
I am not what I am
but what I must be
I know the essence
Because I know none at all
To know joy, ask he who is crying
To know health, ask he who is sick
To know life, ask he who is dying
To know love, as he who is lonely

Come, I grow philosophic, and we must laugh
or we will cry
Think not on me, let me pass, let me go
but let me remember you
I need proof that I am wrong
And let it be said, whatever else I may be
that of all my whispers in the night
one was named Pam.

On the Morning of November 23

On the morning of November 23, 1970, in Houston, Texas, a man who had been shot in the chest went from door to door asking for help. He was found an hour later on the sidewalk by a paperboy. He had taken off his coat, rolled it into a pillow, and lain down to die.

Who died?
Not I, not I
Who died?
Not I

Who killed?
Not I, not I
Who killed?
Not I

Thou shall not murder
Love your neighbor as yourself
Love your enemies and do good to those that hate you
Do unto others as you would have them do unto you
The wages of sin are death
Behold, all have sinned and fallen short of the Glory of God

Who has killed?
I have killed, I have killed
Who has killed?
I have killed

Who had died?
I have died, I have died
Who has died?
I have died.

Over an Antarctic of Clouds

Over an Antarctic of clouds
I flew through sunset's rainbow
From blue to red to darkness

From home to home via Atlanta
The flyboys' way to go.

An Old, Dusty Piano

It was just an old, dusty piano
Long left unused in a darkened corner offstage
He sat on a prop trunk
His melody lured an audience of two on a wooden box
And Nick Weber played
He wore faded jeans, a dirty shirt, long hair, and a mustache
We sat silent before sparking streams of lullaby
And Nick Weber played
At times a vulgar man
Inclined to be obscene
We drank then from his cold, clear mountain spring
And Nick Weber played
Three songs he played
Yes, only three, though one was his own
And for three songs life was pure and good and everyman my friend
Life was peace
When Nick Weber played.

I Saw the Land

I saw the land glowing orange with the sunrise
Tower high, a one-quarter crescent
Above it, love's untwinkling eye
It was morning

The joy of silence, counterpoint
To the cold, clear, that whispered
Now.

Writing

Disconnected thoughts
Stirred by the brain
Congeal into words
In the cold of language.

Loneliness Increases

Loneliness increases
the poetic facility
Moon, June, balloon
Beauty, beauty everywhere
and not a place to shit
Voices creeping from
a babbling brook
Now I know of what
rapists are made.

Avoiding the Question

Love isn't mine to take or give
For I have never loved

Life isn't mine to pass around
For I have never lived
Oh, isn't it sunny
And don't the stars twinkle bright
And isn't the moon sort of upside down
Oh, isn't it sunny tonight
I saw our friend just yesterday
Yes, the Rams are the better team
It's a pity they didn't win
I'll have to leave you now
I've got a story to write
And my guitar I must practice tonight.

Screenplay for an Affair of the Mind

fade in	p	a girl
	a	
haze	s	a glimpse
	s	
focus		class together
	t	
sound	w	hello
	o	
beauty		silent I love you
	y	
diffraction lens	e	no response
	a	
distort	r	another man
	s	
slow fade		she moves on

Walking Song

With cup in hand
I walk this street
a handsome bird
I chance to meet
he passed me by
I passed him up
I took a sip
from my paper cup
my heels they slide
on warm concrete
I'm going home
no one to meet
a dog he bark
he run he jump
up on my knees
I give a grunt
with cup in mouth
I pat his head
wishing I knew
what he said.

Friends Fade

Friends fade
Like a south wind in autumn
But the heart beats hot
Till the tilted globe arights again
And the skull encased gray
Sparks conduction-worn nodes
While forming new circuits
But the old remain forever
Imprinted on my mind.

To Lenelle, Who Let Me Sing with Her

I realize
as do those who hear me
that I shall have to die
and go to heaven
before my voice
becomes angelic
As a certain voice instructor
so aptly put it
I have
the Voice of a Peanut

But even if heaven
should bring me
harmony
it could not purchase
the pleasure
of singing
here
now
at your side

Of things in this world
I love
singing
is one of the few
It is the joy
of a hidden soul
communicating

You allowed me this joy
Your spirit is more beautiful
than your voice.

A Poet's Thanks

Smiles of words
Tears of letters
Embrace the form
Gratitudes of poetry.

Faces on a Freeway

Faces on a freeway
Struggling to go home
But five o'clock is crowding time
And stall, stall, stall
Walkers rushing by them
Getting anywhere
Sole-worn, strong-hearted
Will sup and dine
While people pushing jammers
Rant and rave and whine.

Talking Blues

Once in a while I wail the blues
Once in a while the blues wail me
And once in a while me and the blues
    get together and wail
Me and the talking blues
We're old friends
We been together since way back when
Most o' the time we just talk
    me and the talking blues
But when things get hot
    we wail some red-hot blues

People sometimes ask
>	why I wail the blues
I just pure don't know
>	what else to wail
and I gotta wail
When I'm out of jail
I met the blues in old Carolina
We was introduced
>	by an old black preacher
Who sure knew a lot
>	about earthly woes
And now I knows
Oh Lord, I knows
All about the woes
Having long been discussed
With the talking blues.

Between Raindrops

Were you ever between raindrops
>	falling from the sky
Did you ever catch a cloud
>	as it went passing by
Did you ever stop to think
>	what you owe to the mink
Did you ever think
>	you could get this high
Did you ever see a tree
>	that didn't live for free
Did you ever walk
>	a pine needle road
Did you ever know a creek
>	that didn't gurgle by
Did you ever see a mountain
>	that was not high?

I Haven't

I haven't chased a butterfly
A-drifting in the air
Since I was young
I haven't traced the ripples
That later blew my hair
Since rose-hue left my cheeks
I've stopped caressing rainbows
And riding on white clouds
I've gone away for other things
More permanent than now
I've gone to seek an answer
To the universal why
I've tried to find the words
That make a tear a laugh a cry
I paid with youth for reason
That gives me now a why
Again I go a-chasing
Those orange kites of the sky.

For Richard

Ships
Set sail
To run before the wind
Some to sink at sunrise
Some at noon
And others in the night-dark sea

Cast off! Heave away for we're bound . . .
We're bound
For a storm
For a berg

For a bar
For a mystery

Count the ships that sailed
But never docked
Count the lives born
To be taken
By death the sea
By a breeze
By a heave
By a cloud
By a star

Count no sailor happy
Till his ship has touched
The dock
Count no man safe
Till his voyage has reached
Its end
For remember
We all
Are sailors.

Call to Prayer

Runway lights
Call to prayer
Dark of night
Out there
Chapel flying
In the air
Call to prayer
Call to prayer.

I Must Away

I must away to the cotton fields
      of the hills so green
I must away to the surging waves
      o're the desert sand
I must away
I must away to the silence

I must away from the bustling lights
      of the sky so gray
I must away from the blinding noise
      o're the black brick lands
I must away
I must away to the silence.

She's Going Away

I've got a song in my mind
      that I will never sing
I've got a love in my heart
      that will never wear my ring
She's going away
She's going away
She's going away

Life passes over us
      so they say
Love passes over me
      but for a day
She's going away
She's going away
She's going away

I write my love poem
        hide it in a book
Put my word of love
        where she will never look
She's going away
She's going away
She's going away.

Mona Lisa Dancing

Mona Lisa dancing
        to a tune, to a tune
Mona Lisa dancing
        coming soon, coming soon

I dance, I play, I sing a song
Not too well, but I practice oh so long
He drew mirrored parachutes
And painted silly smiles
I find photon fluxes
And write such silly songs
He and I, she and you
He and I, she and you

Mona Lisa dancing
        to a tune, to a tune
Mona Lisa dancing
        coming soon, coming soon

Can I play the tune?
        coming soon, coming soon.

And When I Awoke

I once had a dream
Or should I say it once had me
I knew how to laugh
And had the world laughing with me
Now, now I'm alone
Waiting to see what will be
Out of a window before my eyes
Memories of dreams are staring at me
Time, time sits alone
Waging its war, collecting its fee
Years, years that are gone
White butterfly come back to me.

WP

I must be the biggest fool
      this side of hell
To fall in love with her
      now
      with her
I cling to the last, rough ledge
      before the crest
      at sunset
Exhausted, almost out of time

She is thin, not beautiful
      her hair is short
She climbs another mountain
      with as little time as I
Yet I fear
She is the second biggest fool
      this side of hell.

Munich, 1972

I hang no symbols on my door
No titles haunt my name
Five rings forever not my battle cry
But today I am a Jew

My father is a Baptist
American I was born
I call humanity my home
So today I am a Jew

Guns are for a world gone mad
Peace for none at all
Christ said Love I am for those who hate
Today I am a Jew.

Should I

Should I make promises
I won't keep
Kiss the teat
But offer no babe to suck?

Song, a Prose Poem

Moon dark light shine on hazel hair rose. Star shine light shine song shine on this love of mine. Sing song to tune play my guitar. I call you call wonder where you are?

Rosebud red rambling on soul feet of clay. Can I call you call on night or day. Rosebud red romance shall call it someday. I sing if you sing we sing on a day. Love with proper connotations, sing your own song. Such sights as a true love sing their own song. Sing song dark moonshine, sing song of today. Sing song to my tune, in harmony me. Call woman ramble, I'm gone someday. My songs have endings, come what may. If you sing with my song know soon I'll be gone.

So sang the young man to his love on a day. He taught her his song and was soon gone away. Now sings she a ramble, and rambles a day by the dark of the moonshine and the light of the song. Sing song red ramble, I'll sing you a lay to keep you from moonshine and the cold of the day. Are you hazel hair rose all gone away? Sing not by the moonshine, for he's all gone away.

Her Breast Lay Lightly

Her breast lay lightly in the curve of the guitar
Her voice gently on my ear
We sang unafraid
As sparking fingers danced on strings
We courted in melody
Loved in rhythm
And grew in time
Life is not a song
The song is life.

Another Song

For it's known that I'll be going
And it's gone that I'll be knowing
And I would not have you swimming in
      the rivers of my mind
For the currents there are flowing, they are deep
and they are going, they will drag you down
and drown and how much better if you kneel upon
the sand that forms the shore and dip your hand
and quench your thirst therein and know that it was fine
For it's known that I'll be going
And it's gone that I'll be knowing
And I would not have you swimming in
      the rivers of my mind
For the rivers they are flowing, they are gone
and they are going past the point that you are knowing
leaving but a stream there flowing in a crevice
of your mind Ah but drink and leave the river flowing
seaward seaward it is going leaving but a memory
of a water clear and fine
For it's known that I'll be going
And it's gone that I'll be knowing
And I would not have you swimming in
      the rivers of my mind.

Incomplete

It's hot as a plasma
You can see the pain
      dripping off his brow
His work, like threading needles
      while sitting on a star going nova
Is made repetitious by failure
      And boring by despair.

Three Relative Quanta

c plus c equals c
1 plus 1 equals 1
Bother me not with reason old man
The universe has its own logic

Lambda equals h over p sheds light upon light
Uniting contradiction
Its existence forcing the world
To change its mind

Delta p delta x equals h bar over 2 means I am not sure
Where I am, or how fast I am going where
But I think maybe I can guess
How far off course I am.

Just Now

Just now, I just want to hold you
     in my arms
That's all
Just to lie in the grass, my arm
     under your neck
Your head
     on my shoulder
Just now that's all I ask
     I ask
Warm sun, cool breeze
Just your warmth against
     my side
That's all I ask
     Just now.

Spring-Sun

The lilacs are a-blooming
Filling the air with grape Kool-Aid
And for those of us
Who live on the border of life
Where flowers are not
       pretty, sweet-smelling things
But miracles
It is time to sing
Our soft, sad tune of blue joy.

Pray for Love

The flickering candle-light lit her face
I touched her hand, it opened
and I lay mine within
In a silent circle of friends
I felt her fire-goldened hair
fall on my hand as she bowed her head
Pray for love
Aye, we prayed for that and more
with laughter, song, and silence
If there had been room
we would have danced for sorrow
and cried for joy
Pray for love
Searching through God for each other
God is love, and love was there, all around
In the silent circle of a hundred spoken prayers
I wanted to stroke her hair, touch her cheek
Say I love you to every person there
I hit her, hurt her
Insulted every soul
Eli, Eli, Lama Sabachthani?
"And they'll know we are Christians by our love"
Pray for love.

Beethoven's Child

(To a Musician Going Deaf)

Such silence you must hear
        amidst your Bach
Such silence, such silence
        feeling your cello's strings
Haunted, haunted by soundless harp

Does Beethoven's madness
        frighten your scarred ears
Such silence, such silence
        behind every note
            every song
            every sound
        of night or man

What melody, what tune, what sound
        would you play
        would you hear
If it were the last
        before again
        such silence.

Rain

The cat on the cliffs is staring
        cold and wet
Under the tree beating rain
        on the ground
Cat fur clouds cover the sky
        causing the rocks to shiver
The sun sleeps early
        but the stars never rise

The earth shrinks
      in the mist
And distances are gone
      when it rains.

Another Poem From Lenelle

You can't by love
at least not a Joske's
or anywhere else in San Antonio
I've looked
Because, you see
in my own strange way
I love you
And so on Love's anniversary
I wanted to give you love
But they didn't have any
Only "Ode d' Luv," or
"Love's Scent" or
"LOVE, in fourteen-carat gold"
But no love
Not even at Sears
So I settled for this signet
and some wax
to seal
whatever you might wish.

My Name Is the Beloved

My name is the Beloved
I was born in the land
  of the three Tygers
I grew amid the swamps
   by the great ocean
   in the soft pines
   near the wide river
My ancestors
   from the cool mountains
   from the hot plains
Grew cotton, tobacco, and corn
   preached, taught, and farmed
The land is in their blood
They are where they have been since they came
Family after family
Generation after generation
They are here
And I am here

I wish I was in Texas.

I Lost a Part of Me Today

I lost a part of me today
She went to Chicago
When she gets back
I'll be gone
(That's all)?

Camping

Looking at myself in the bottom
       of a thermos jug top
I see only me
       sitting in my van
       listening to a dog bark
       remembering how good
             water tastes
             night looks
             blankets feel
             life is.

Untitled

I've been reading poetry
Now I thought to live some
Lying by shade tree
       on the bed grass
       under blanket sun
       to music squirrel
Falling asleep amid the rhymes.

Sometimes

Sometimes
I feel like
I'm just passing through
Not really making a dent
    in the sheet metal of life
Using a sort of quantum tunneling effect
    to go in and out
Without changing anybody's
    energy level
Like Maxwell's Un-Demon
    frittering away the ordered energy
    of a neon atom in a star
Unnoticed in the mass
Unseen in the brilliance
    of a googillion lesser lights.

Light

A ball of light
Went passing by
And went and waved at me
It waved so hard
It waved itself
As I could plainly see
The packet waved
And bounced away
As solid as could be.

Poet's Prayer

Our face is back into the wind
All the nonessentials overboard
We are down to fighting weight
Stripped body and soul
Pleasures denied
Friends and lovers cast out
Left lonely and in sorrow
They are
What I gave up
Denied
Those who would love
So I could stand
Silent and alone
Their forgiveness I dare not ask
But
If I do not become
The Greatest Poet
In the history of the world
God forgive me.

Or So I'm Told

Used to be
(or so I am told)
Women's bodies were expensive
Purchasable only at the price of
      candles by dinner light
      false words
      gold rings
(I'm not sure about all this)
      relatives
      and responsibilities

But along with the body you got
      cooking
      cleaning
      mothering
(I'm not sure I believe all this either)
      supporting
      and loving (Remember that word)

Now
(or so I understand)
Female bodies are
Two for a nickel
Three cents if you only want one
But most, like toasters
      last only a year or two
      (if not dropped)
      and come without
      the extra frills.

March 17th

On March 17th
They were flying
Kites
As I walked by
On my way to the
Zoo
To see what
The other animals
Do
In spring.

Heed Me Well

Heed me well my youthsome friend
There's not much life in a life of sin
Nor much to say and savor in
      a wordless world
And little joy in a friendless end
Sell a soul a penny
A pocket full of rye
I gave mine to a friend
To hold until I die
I'm going home on the morning train
Get your ticket at the station
      For the Rock Island Line
Life is like a thumbnail
I heard a man once say
To use it, you gotta file it
Grind away, grind away.

Damn It

I'm in love, damn it
The hell I am!
Why don't I call her
Because I don't know what to say
I must be in love; this is my third poem today
I am not Robert Burns
I walk the neon streets like Tom Wolfe
I'm not him either
I am David Davis, and there's this girl . . .
She's not even very pretty
Of course not
So what?
So why am I crying
Hell if I know
I don't usually curse
I don't usually cry either
Which proves?
Nothing.

To What Shall I Sing

To what shall I sing
She has no beauty the eye can behold
Her voice no angel's trill
But yet, but yet
No fortune comes with her kiss
No genius with those arms
But yet, but yet
Her soul, perhaps?
No
I know her little
Her personality
No

But yet, but yet
Her body?
It is small
Her love?
But slow and weak
But yet, but yet
I shall sing.

Mayhaps

Mayhaps I am in love
If so
I stand amazed
At how little difference it makes
My lips have not changed
      since her kiss
My hands altered not
      from the feel of her
No one notices a change in me
Except
I cry now and then
My phone bill has gone up
And I never study on Saturday night
Such a little difference

The world should cry.

There's a Fire

There's a fire in my boots
Another in my thighs
And a third in my brain
I hear that in hell one burns
But is not consumed
(And I thought I was in San Antonio)
Midnight cool desert sand
A touch of teat to lip
Enough glory to pay the bills
Would be water to my soul
What I get is a dorm room
Friday night homework
And bit parts
Oh hell.

Silence

Silence
Silence
We loved in silence
Then in silence ceased
Once in a while someone takes a knife
      and cuts the silence
And his own heart
We could have spoken
There were pauses between the kisses
Or later
Or before
Either of us
But silence
Silence.

Questions

Can a man doubt God
while a butterfly flickers about his toes
Can he shake a nut and hear a tree rattle
and say I am alone
Can the sun shine on one tree bud
and deny life
Can the green grass say
I am a dream
Or a spring wind
call itself chance?

No, I think not.

Vacation, '69–'70

Blue sky, gray sky
Sun shine through the rain
She has gone now
Left me alone again
How much to fly to New York City
How much to fly away
Christmas is a long time coming
When your love is far away
This much time must pass now
Till my blue sun shine
Next year is a long time coming
When your love is far away
When your love is far away.

Lonely Girl

I write only phrases
Sing only snatches of song
Think philosophical thoughts
    without beginning or end

Lonely girl
Shall I come and stay with you
Lonely girl
Would you want me to
Lonely girl

I am certainly not in love
Just growing up a bit mayhaps
Just finding I have a body
    to go with my mind

Lonely girl
Shall I come and stay with you
Lonely girl
Would you really want me to
Lonely girl

It's only puppy love between two old dogs
Two not-very-beautiful people
Two wallflowers, last in line for the dance
    just now getting their first foxtrot

Ye gods! Why didn't somebody
    teach me to dance?

To a Teacher

What's the right thing to say
to a girl you've just kissed
      and hugged and felt in
         various and assorted places?
What's the right thing to say
after an hour of sweat and
      heavy breathing and mouth-
        to- mouth resuscitation?

I didn't know it would come so
Dinner, a movie, Kool-Aid in her apartment
A kiss or two was all my hope
But as we sat side-by-side on her sofa
There was this lull in the conversation
I kissed her, she kissed me
And an hour later we were still
      compressing the space between us

I could have held her all night
But my arm went to sleep
      under her head
And besides, she had to get up
      in the morning to plant flowers
So we unwrapped and parted

But next Saturday, or even this Wednesday
I'll be back
Still looking for the right thing to say.

Response

From the fire in our hearts
The smoke of our prayers
Rises up to you, oh Lord.

Love Song

Something somewhere fell apart
And so did we
I don't know why
It's a mystery
But this I know
I wish I had some glue
For pieces of a memory
Remind me of what used to be
On days when life was one
And not just pieces broken by the sun
The fragments of our love
Are scattered here and there
Some upon the wind
Some upon the air
Some upon the rain
The only tears we share
Oh will these shards
Again be ever joined
Or crumble into dust
And dirt and bits of sand
For something somewhere fell apart
And so did we
I don't know why
It's a mystery
But this I know
I wish I had some glue.

For Taking a Chance

Well I wouldn't know
How far to go
How far to reach and take it
And I wouldn't pay

Two cents a day
To dance in your sideshow
If we're gonna stay
If we're gonna lay
Down and do it now
Please let me know
What is the payment
For taking a chance, for taking this dance
      for putting my hand right to it
If I'm gonna play
This game your way
Then read me the rules on through it
And what kind of blow
Could lay me down low
And leave me astray
I'm taking it slow
Cause this is no show
For getting on in a day
So please go and say
What is the payment
For taking a chance, for risking the lance
      for starting to go right to it?

Ode to Navel Lint

That seems to come out of the air
And settle down there
Mist navel and hair
And must be dug out every night.

Ah Life

Ah life, thou art a whisper
spoken softly
heard by but few
then quickly gone.

I Am

I am by nature a pessimist
by influence a cynic
by necessity a stoic
and by God a Christian.

Scraps of Paper, Containing Words

This really isn't a poem
It lacks form
It has no sense
Just words lying on paper
Scraps of paper containing words

I wanna go home
Where the wind blows
Where the grass grows
Where the river flows
I wanna go home

Words, symbols
Standing for thoughts
Long forgotten
Always remembered

I wanna go home
Where the birds fly
Where the streams lie
Where the crickets cry
I wanna go home

A meaningless thing
Words lying on paper
Scraps of paper containing words.

Creativity Flows

Creativity flows like concrete too long in the sun
Thoughts ripple like waves in a mosquito pool
I run with the throngs in Death Valley sands
Life blossoms like a lily in December
I forge after dreams like sound chasing light
And am welcomed like a king to a new-found, still empty land.

A Life in Reverse

Perfume and chewing gum
The ten-year-old teenagers
Swing to their mother's beat
Firs and fancy hairdos
Jewels and beaus
Plays and dances
The cultured little rich kid
Goes steady at twelve
And wild at seventeen.

Beauty Is a Butterfly

Beauty is a butterfly
Skimming the uncut grass
Spring is tapping on my doorstep
Knocking on my window
Pounding on my eyes
Warm winds sound reveille
And flowers form a sea
Trees don their uniforms
And a little bird is being born.

Tucson Poetry (1974-76)

Fill the Valley with Ditches

Fill the valley with ditches
And let the Good Lord work
God'll put the water
Where there was none before
If you'll just fill the valley with ditches
And let the Good Lord work
Well, as Elisha told Jehoshaphat
When the water ran out
God'll give you plenty
Without any doubt
But you gotta do your bit
Just to show that you believe
You got to be ready
Before you can receive
Fill the valley with ditches
And let the Good Lord work
God'll put the water
Where there was none before
If you'll just fill the valley with ditches
And let the Good Lord work
Well, the lesson's still true
The moral's still plain
If you want to get a miracle
You got to do more than pray for rain
If you want a drink of blessing
You got to hold out your cup
You got to fill the valley with ditches
And let the Good Lord work.

Leaf-Filtered Light

Leaf-filtered light
finds my window
shading paper
that stares at me
blankly, begging
for words.

My Dreams Are Lying on the Floor

My dreams are lying on the floor
Punch drunk
Bleeding
The count has started
The ring is silent
There is no crowd
Only the roaring in my ears
I think about getting up
But can't remember which direction up is
I consider it may be safer to stay down
But I'm afraid someone will come
      and sweep the floor
Rolling over is a possibility
But where is the edge?
I decided to stay down for eight
Then try to get up
But I can't hear the count.

Dress Rehearsal Rag

It's a dress rehearsal rag way up here
        in West Virginia
And I'm sitting in the corner
        trying to remember my lines
The director up and shouts
        "One more time"
It's a dress rehearsal rag way up here
        in West Virginia

Well, the set ain't so bad
        but glory what the lights reveal
And the star is so nervous
        he just threw up his last meal
It's a dress rehearsal rag way up here
        in West Virginia
And I'm sitting in the corner
        trying to remember my lines
The director up and shouts
        "Well, one more time"
It's a dress rehearsal rag way up here
        in West Virginia

Well, the good old leading lady
        she hit her cue right on time
But her costume went and split
        right down to the bust line
And I think I saw the costumer
        heading out the back door
And I'm not really sure
        we're going to see him no more
It's a dress rehearsal rag way up here
        in West Virginia
And I'm sitting in the corner
        trying to remember my lines

The director up and shouts
        "Get it right this time"
It's a dress rehearsal rag way up here
        in West Virginia

Well, I guess the folks up here
        got a right to see a show
But it sure ain't New York
        or even Chicago
I been to LA
        but I couldn't make a dime
If I could just go back to Dallas
        Work for Mr. Baker one more time
It's a dress rehearsal rag way up here
        in West Virginia
And I'm sitting in the corner
        trying to remember my lines
The director up and shouts
        "I quit"
It's a dress rehearsal rag way up here
        in West Virginia.

You'd Think

You know, you'd think the sun would burn
        the mountains blow away
        the seas fill with sand
        and dreams die

I was told they do

But I've looked
        and watched
        and waited

I can't see it.

To Bobbie

Tell the broken lady
After the Potter has put her back together
That I love her
And pray for her
And that the fire in my heart
Sends the smoke of my prayers
Soaring up to heaven

And I know
One day I will come
And play for her
And she will sing for me
Again.

A Short Poem Having to Do with Christmas in the Home

It was a pot-bellied stove
    that held the center of the room
        at Grandma's house
The Christmas tree was over in the corner
    leaning against the wall
        so as not to fall
It had been cut with an axe
    not a saw, and axe-cut trees
        always seem to lean
Christmas morning we had to wait for Dad to get the stove going
    before we could hop out of our warm beds
        and run down to open our presents
I was the oldest child, so I was the one
    who got up and woke Dad, then jumped back into bed
        while he went to start the coal fire
After presents, we dressed, then ran to the kitchen
    where Grandma was already scrambling eggs
        and Grandpa sat with his Bible open

while he was alive. Later, Dad would do the reading
>   but he was always late getting dressed
>   >   and the eggs got cold while we waited

Some Christmases we got the shepherds from Luke
>   others the wise men from Matthew
>   >   and once Dad read from Isaiah

When the hour got decent Mom would let Sis and me
>   run visit the neighbors to see what toys
>   >   they had gotten that year

Then in the afternoon we would all drive to an aunt's house
>   for a big family dinner with relatives
>   >   from all over that we never saw any other time

Grandma and Grandpa are dead now, and Christmas trees
>   are bought in stores, houses come with central heating
>   >   and I'm the one who only gets home for Christmas

And all that's natural and part of growing up I guess
>   but when I go out to buy my Christmas tree
>   >   I still look for one that leans.

We All Go Home Alone

We all go home alone
After all the rehearsals
After all the performances
After all the parties
After all the sweating together
After all the joying together
After all the crying together
After all the living/loving/laughing together
After the show is over
We all go home alone.

On the Impossibility of Communication

In the first place
We don't even speak the same language
We both call what we speak English
(Which is ridiculous since neither one of us has
      ever been within a thousand miles of England)
But I speak a sort of Carolina Southern Baptist
      Preacher's Kid Physicist Dramatist dialect
And you speak, well, whatever it is you speak

And in the second place
I'm a man and you're a woman
Which may mean we're equal
But doesn't mean we're the same
Some sort of hormone difference
So that while we inhabit the same planet
We're not the same creatures
We do not think alike, it's been proven
By scientists

And in the third place
Which may be due to cultural differences
Or upbringing or body rhythms
Or simply that we don't live together
Twenty-four hours a day, but at any rate
I just don't understand you.

The Coming and Going of the Rains

The coming and going of the rains
by which we live
are two
Moisture
to feed our streams and plants
so we may drink and eat
Friendship
to feed our souls and minds
so we may cry and laugh
Without one
Our bellies bloat and bones stick out
Without the other
we stare at space and doubt ourselves

I seem to have hit a drought.

Rosemary Died Last Night

Rosemary died last night
From coke on a ride
From wanting to glide
Somebody was a cut-up
And Mary got the joke
She took a bad toke
Someone liked his party spiked
So Rose is all gone
A wheel through her bone

Next?

Houses I Have Seen in Passing

Chorus:　　　You never really know
　　　　　　No, you never really know
　　　　　　Some may come and some may go
　　　　　　And you never really know
　　　　　　First they're here
　　　　　　Then they're gone with the morning

Verse:　　　 Like the night-lit window shade
　　　　　　People wear before their eyes
　　　　　　And all you see is paint and
　　　　　　　　and windowpane
　　　　　　No, you never see inside
　　　　　　In the rooms where people hide
　　　　　　So you never really know

Chorus:　　　You never really know
　　　　　　No, you never really know
　　　　　　Some may come and some may go
　　　　　　And you never really know
　　　　　　First they're here
　　　　　　Then they're gone with the morning

Verse:　　　 And it's a little cold outside
　　　　　　But inside the fire has died
　　　　　　And the glow is just
　　　　　　　　electrical illusion
　　　　　　No, there is no warmth inside
　　　　　　Those that hide have died
　　　　　　And you never really know

Chorus:　　　You never really know
　　　　　　No, you never really know
　　　　　　Some may come and some may go

And you never really know
First they're here
Then they're gone with the morning.

I Have a Picture

I have a picture of her face
A tape of her sounding voice
But of her scent when she lay
    near me naked
Of her cherry earlobe taste
    tucked between my lips
Of her touch and scratching
    of my palm
I have nothing, only memories

Technology, you have failed me.

When You Get Right Down to It

When you get right down to it
I'm just a Southern Baptist
    from South Carolina
And a Preacher's Kid at that
It's a wonder I'm not still
    down in the swamps
Praying and reading the KJV
Instead of driving life into a corner
    in Arizona
Working in the unholy of unholies
    the Theatre
Voicing a mild heresy now and then
    at the BSU

Isn't God wonderful!

The Big Black Silent Night Blues

The Big Black Silent Night Blues
Snow down on the Christmas soul
Far from the family fire
Jesus songs to the not-at-home
Are not hymns to joy
But bawling blues to a bastard boy
Born in a barn
Who, like the singer now, cried
Because he was far
From his father's hearth-warm home.

God's Church of the Lonely

The congregation of God's church of the lonely
Worships at night in the streets
Separately
Searching for some soul to save
Themselves
Befriended only by God
They search for someone to complete the triangle
For, let's face it folks,
God, for all the other wonderful things He is,
Is not a very good lay.

No Lies

Tell me no lies
Sing me no songs of disguise
And I'll take you by the hand
Show you where my soul began
Lead you into my own land
Make you woman to my man

Tell me no lies
Sing me no songs of disguise
And before it is done
We will become one
Two souls in the sun
Watching our lives be unspun

Tell me no lies
Sing me no songs of disguise
And when things are end
Only memories to send
Another's songs to begin
We'll have no songs to rescind

Tell me no lies
Sing me on songs of disguise.

The Chrysanthemums Bloomed

The chrysanthemums bloomed
the day I was born
twenty-four years ago
my mother said
she remembers, she says
I don't, but I suppose
if one has to be born
a good day to do it
is the day
the chrysanthemums bloomed.

So It Ends

So it ends
love left
behind becoming
letters languishing
into infrequency
into never
into memory.

Why People Got Married

He was beginning to understand
Why people got married
It wasn't for sex, or love
It was out of fear
Fear of silence
The silence of being alone

He sat on his bed in his cell-size apartment
Wearing only his underwear
Letting the radio hold the silence at bay
Marriage was a guarantee, he knew
A guarantee that there would be someone to speak at
To touch when
To break the silence of
A living together with a lease
It cost more than a whore every Saturday night
But there wasn't a time limit
The problem being, he could afford neither
His pocket could not pay a wife
Or his soul a whore
And in the dating-mating game of unliberated man
Every woman began as whore
To be paid in food, drink, and song

A few could become almost wife
But that costs time and freedom more
So he sat
Semi-naked, the struggling writer-actor
Caressing only words
Playing great lovers on the stage
Writing great loves double-spaced in triplicate
Living no loves at all

It had not always been thus
Once the hairs below the navel
Had been his to entwine
The erect nipples his to enfold
The heaving female form his to engulf
But he was a moral man
Who, never knowing love
Believed it yet
Not loving, but considering her future
Of as much right as his
He left and bid her not come
So gone ten thousand miles
He sat
Considering the silence
Caressing his words
Remembering to forget

He had heard that prisoners
Kept too long in solitary
Soon began to love silence
Need the isolation
He wasn't sure he believed that
But he thought he might find out.

'Tis Not Heaven

'Tis not heaven I hold here
But my hand
That dances fire
And spins
A universe away.

To the Vietnam Vet

I, 1-Y and scholarly
Far from a war
I knew as a political issue
Knew there must be bullets
At the end of a ballot
But I never saw the pain
Till I heard the whine
Of a twelve-volt wheelchair
Watched a frozen-sided man
Play basketball
And saw the fear-averted eyes
Of a man who never spoke
Of two years of his life.

Mathematics

Of girls I have kissed
That count
But three

Of nipples I have sucked
Since youth
But four

Of cunts I have cuddled
In hand
But one

Of people I have loved
Not one
Not one.

Finger Sketches

Finger sketches in sea-shore sand
Lives are left to be
And only one drops a pebble by
Or casts a rock on sand

And one a bit of shell of sea
Or sprig of dune-grass green
The rest are soon washed on by
As the wave-roar dulls their scream.

On Falling

When you are six and zero
And padded little like I
Falling
Is not fun.

Oh, for a Job up in Heaven

Oh, for a job up in heaven
Where they publish all that I write
Where angels applaud each new sonnet
And God is an autograph hog

I hate the hum of electrics
That impatiently wait to be typed
While I sit and stare
At the end of my hair
Praying for something to write

Wipe the Morning

Wipe the morning from your eyes
Greet the dawn with the sounds of yawning
Clear the head with the day's first sneezes
And try to forgive the sun for rising.

Once This Was Mine

Once this was mine
     to hold in my hand
     a dance of flame
     across a stage
A wind across a mind

I put my torch to paper
     and prayed that
     it would burn
I spent the wind tomorrow
     and took the time
     to yearn

Someday my flame will
      dance across a stage
        in my hand or another
My wind will sweep
      another's mind
        by book, by song, by time
By play, by verse, or mind.

Hear the Silence

Hear the silence
Tapping, Tapping
Be Aware, Be Aware
Note the quiet
Leaking, Leaking
Do you care, Do you care
Feel the empty
Slipping, Slipping
Do you dare, Do you dare
Know the nothing
Pounding, Pounding
Beware, Beware.

I'm Going

I'm going
      riding the plains
           of my memory
      climbing the mountains
           of my mind
      sailing a sea
           I sailed but yesterday
When I left today behind

I've been saddlesore
           footsore and
           seasick
    of a pain
Of a pain
      was the time
But Then is clearer
         sweeter
         bitter now
For it's gone
      like footprints
      left behind.

Feel the Night

Feel the night
Lie with me
We'll find a shadow in the dark
Hide from the stark quarter moon
In a grass hollow below
    the shadow sound
    the fleeing photon
Feel me
Lie with the night
We'll find a silence in the dark
Hide from the mind of our eye
In a caressing touch below
    the shadow thought
    the fleeing mind.

Search

Search for any wandering soul
Find only fallen men
Look for one longing free
Discover men loving cells
Seek bits of matching mind
Perceive only far stars and space.

Mauldin Songs (1976-78)

The Wind is Empty

The wind is empty
Calling no names
Singing no songs
Crying no tears
Only doing what wind does
Rustling leaves
Mussing hair
Blowing rain
It is I who calls
And sings and cries

Soft as the breeze that made them
These mountains
Lie like a woman on the ground
Sinuous, seductive
Opening to me
Tempting me

My Night

My night is but a star's wink
So, at times, I take a shorter view
Take the effect of wind
      upon a mountain
Some say the wind wears
      The mountain down
I know better
It is the wind that bends.

Too Soon Silence

I must seek out my soul again
I lost it on a ride
      that left me dizzy
      distant, down
Watching life whirl
      away from me
      as I was spun, run, done
Left lone, a bone shed
      of its meat.

Silence

There is too much silence here
      too long
I grow deaf of it
No longer able to hear
      the friendly word
      the chummy cue
      the too-light tint tone
          of love

Too soon silence shall
      I hear all
Despite how loud the cry.

The Car

I'm wearing out
Like a car run past its warranty
The wear is beginning to show
I squeak and rattle
I take more gas
        and get fewer miles
I'm out of style, a bit dented
        and starting to rust
I need new tires, some engine work
        and a paint job
I just hope they don't trade me in
        on a new model.

Suddenly Old

My father made out his will today
He told me he felt it was time
So why is it I
Who feels suddenly old?

Hate

I have hated few men in my life
I hate one now
If he were not so about me
        he would be a pitiable thing
        dumb, troubled, deficient
But he forces his presence upon me
        with threats and stones
I fear only the stones
        but I fear them enough
                to hate him.

Cruelties That Walk

There are cruelties that walk the earth
Who falsely claim the name of man
They are not
Only half men
The half all have and most hide
Is all they have
Their pain is our pain
      for they inflict themselves
           upon us
With a gun
      or a knife
           or a word.

Memories of a Flying Horse

I wonder if the pixie has gone out
The impish smile I used to know
Leaving walking talking shell
Of life and love I knew as girl.

If I Am Too Late

I wonder if I am too late
If the world will go to pieces now
Before I have my shot at it
Before I can conquer it and soar
Will it fall from under me
Never caring how high I might have flown
If it had but stood solid as I leaped.

Dunes

I remember the dunes again
Standing on the sea grass
      looking over the sea glass
            rippled by the sun
The dunes pound into the waves
Rushing away in the foam
      like a life
            rippled by the sun.

IF

If I never wrote again
What would I say today
How a flower grew
Where the pain ends
No
Here the tears begin.

We Talk

We talk
      face to face
And warm each other
      with our breath
But that is all
      that passes
            between us.

Patriotism

There is a little black girl
        in my yard
Singing the Battle Hymn
        of the Republic
As she rides her tricycle
        up and down the walk
I don't know why
        she sings it now
But it is certainly nice to know
        That patriotism is not dead.

Silent Nights

Silent nights
Crying in the streets
The lights blurred
        in the winked-back tears
Scribbling verses
        on notepads
Dripping emotions
        on pavement
Crying in the shock
        of not being hated
Of not being turned away
        of maybe
Just maybe
        being loved.

Flecks of Light

Like flecks of light
    the silver hair
        that rode her bosom
Young she was
    the goose down unruffled
        by gander hands
Just a glimpse
    over low-cut into gap
        of refracted shimmer
The eyes-to-hands promise
    of future delight.

The Music of My Soul

They broke the music of my soul
Left my life a pentameter of four measures
An irregular iambic of pointless counterpoint
A sonnet with thirteen rhymes
I cannot sing a song without time
Nor march to a beatless drum
But what use is a sprightly tune
In a city of monotone souls.

A Woman's Room

I had forgotten the scent of a
    woman's room
Having lived too long in my own
    company
Had forgotten that colors
    so cacophonous about me

Could be blended
       into melody
I had forgotten that furniture
       could float
Not stone stand like my
       solid chests
That rooms, like women, could put beauty
       to use.

On Baptist Women

Brains and boobs in a Baptist are hard to find
I've known a few with boobs
Fewer still with brains
But Baptists with both boobs and brains
Are evidently a contradiction of terms.

Walking Warm

When walking warm from heated house
to still, cold night for minutes seems
tis not so cold on windless eve
till voices from the windows ring
of crying child and scolding sire
of reviling rants and rude remains
and suddenly tis cold it seems.

Soldiers

They are soldiers
They die, if necessary
When the time comes
If someone has to, they do

To preserve democracy
      they live in a dictatorship
To preserve freedom
      they become bondsmen
To preserve peace
      they fight wars
To preserve life
      they die

It's a strange world, sometimes.

Call

Call the sons and lovers
      to sing my song
Call the wives and weepers
      to play my tune
Call me in the morning
      and I'll be gone

            It's strange
                  if all you can remember
                        of a lover
            Is the way
                  she scratched
                      your hand

It's stranger still
        in the morning light
                to sing no song
If the wet green dew
        on the copper hue
                shows no sign of going
If all you can say
        of the child-fresh day
                is time will soon be blowing

                                  I knew a girl
                                  who disappeared
                                  leaving her parents
                                  unknowing
                                  sad to say
                                  for a year and a day
                                  till they give up
                                  the thought of hoping.

On a hill far away
        stood an old something or other
                also a sign of a going
Sing a song of sixpence
        pocket full of rye
I won't get you to the universe
        but you might get out of town

                                  I get a letter now and then
                                  stamped gone away
                                  for a year and a day
                                  Say, how do you know
                                  a forwarding address
                                  when you don't know
                                  where you're going?

I Left Her

I left her in a drugstore
In Yuma, Arizona
Waiting for her ship to come in
Which, being in the middle of a desert
Is a strange place to wait for a ship
Unless California drops off
But never mind that
I found out she had disappeared
       later
Searching for a sea
       I guess
Meanwhile, I sit surrounded
       by plaster-white walls
Uncolored by posters or prints
Untouched by nail or tape
Facing myself
Wondering if she will sail by
And tack something up.

The Way the Rivers Run

The way the rivers run
       over the baseball field
In the spring rain
       seems to me to say
No land is flat
No place serene
       but cut by coursers
       usually silent
       and unseen.

The Limits of My Sole

The limits of my sole
      (not that one, the one I walk upon)
are clear marked
by rings of dirt
upon my sandal top
where, as I walked
to here and there
a grain or two of
wheresoever I had been
crept o're the edge
and clung to the wet
sweat leather leaving
line about my toes
a grain or two for every step
with every breath or move
a bit of world had come to me
and laid down a telling trail
defining, delining
the limits of my soul.

I Heard a Cry

I heard a cry
a silent cry
of Kathy, skinny Kathy
black and blue
by father's belt
of rounder Pat
in far-off town
too young to wed
or wife to be
whose sister's spouse
found one night alone
and left with virtue parted
I heard a cry
of Nancy Jean
fat old friend
whose husband left
her to lonely cry
How does love start
like a horse in fright
to gallop at the thunder
in the sky storm slashing
I heard a cry
a silent cry
it was I
it was I.

Carbondale Poems 1978-80

This Is No

This is no moon for howling
'Tis but three quarter done
But the song on my heart is a-laden
And I feel my season has come

This is no rock on a mountain
'Tis but a lake by a stone
But the yearn in my heart is a-yowling
And I feel my life starting to moan

Brother wolf, under sky, cunning and sly
Dark of night, he and I, crying so high
Home is to moonward
It must be so
For so we prowl
Down here below

This is no moon for howling
'Tis but three quarters done
But the strains my heart is a-chanting
Are of cold darkly nights like a bone.

Loneliness

A tree with no sparrow
A wife with no womb
A man who does not know he snores.

Money, but No Words

Money, but no words
my father sends me

blank letters enfolding
federal reserve green
a somehow insufficient care
like the smiles women give me
when they would give nothing else
is it any wonder then
that my wallet is full
and my life is empty.

I Think I Could Live in a Harem

I think I could live in a harem
        and not get laid
Even the eunuchs, sterile old men
        with high voices
If they could but partly function
        were in great demand
I would get but smiles

Nights, in a college town, with
        ten thousand emancipated women
Young and far from home, with
        X-rated movies and
Sexual assertion classes in every
        paper, I sit with Buck
And Roy and an old mule

Excuse the self-pity, but we all must
        have some comfort
And to my great puzzlement, it is still
        only a blanket
That warms my bed, and only
        a video beauty that
Talks me to sleep.

Big Things

Big things I understand
It's the little things I don't
Stars are comprehensible to me
Even glimpses of eternity
Truth, justice, are easy to see
People are not so simple
        to be understood by dolts like me
Do flowers understand bees?
Or rivers, seas?
If the space-time curve
        seems in my sight
Or quark's vibrations
        like ABCs
Why is a smile
        such a puzzle?
If an osculating curve
        I can calculate
And Schrödinger's Equation
        derive
Why is a wink
        such a mystery
With a TI 9000 Programmable
And a CRC Handbook besides
Why is the curve of a thigh
        still so damnable?

This Halloween

No one came this Halloween
No ghosts or goblins at my door
No "Trick or Treat!" was ever screamed
Though I had fine, wrapped candy
        from the store

I have heard of men so isolate
They could count no friend on Christmas's date
And of a few so solitary
No enemy desired their territory

But can a man alone so be
With neither friend nor enemy
That on witches' eve no goblin ghoul
Or soulless spirit, for trick or treat
For fair or foul, will dark his door
With candy corn sitting on the shelf?

To Write Again

How good it is to write verse again
Or at least what I, in my non-English major's
      loose way with a term, call verse
To cut a tear on a scrap of tree
      leave a line across tomorrow's mind
      edge a smile of graphite lead
It salves a scrape or two
      chinks an empty crack
      cools a rough and bleeding sore.

Winter

The winter burned brown trees
      stare back at me
Barren and empty
Dormant now, waiting out
      another winter
They know, in these iced months
      of frozen life
That this too will pass
My soul is not so sure.

A Man

A man of whom it can
      be truly said
He has no enemies
And fewer friends.

Not a Sonnet

I cannot, though I try, a sonnet write
It galls my bones a bit when poets meet
And cry aloud their lines of verse so tight
I often sink my head and seek the street
My pen I've tried to fit in many forms
But will not stay contained within the rule
So seems I fail if judged by any norms
And my wild muse a lass that will not school
But when my lines their own awry form find
And thought define the nature of my verse
Let no scholar of rigid eye or mind
Call me to task or leave for me a curse
If I to end my lines a curvéd smile
Or rounded tear or twisted pun compile.

Symphony of Lights

A symphony of lights streaks
      out before me
and to the right, red, and
      to the left, white
green overhead, with occasional
      hints of yellow

The cracked window whistle
    of the van
    winds past the ear
The closet liberal
    from South Carolina
thinks of taking off clothes
and all the uses and meanings
    of this pedestrian act
But tonight I am riding
    to see the play
and cannot walk
    to my thoughts.

It's Ten O'Clock

It's ten o'clock, and
    my car is falling apart
    my stomach is eating itself
    and my poetry won't scan
The mechanic I saw
    went off laughing
My doctor has a limp
    and may be dying
And my weak lines
    don't even have strong stress
My father lost his job
My sister got laid off
And my syllables don't count
My income just went up
    to the poverty level
I haven't got a friend
    in the world
And my poetry will just
    have to take care
    of itself.

Aspic

Aspic
Tastes like something
My mother would want me to eat
I was served some
Last night at a friend's
For dinner
Covered with homemade
Mayonnaise
(the aspic that is)
But I'm less experienced
Than she
And I guess it showed
My aspic was left half eaten.

Going for Stamps

Walking through the Illinois August green
Watching life grasshopper at my sandaled toes
Sprouting blue and yellow butterfly flutterbys
Smelling the farmer's hay and green melons
Wondering what a city is doing here.

There's Someone in Here

There's someone in here
hiding
nursing his dreams
knowing nothing hurts
    like a dream come true
living in pain already
fearing.

Dissidents

Every now and then
a brave man
stands
and quotes Thoreau
Ah Mother Russia
with your Siberian cold heart
why do they love you
why have so many
given so much
and gotten so little
in return
Why are your lovers
to your cold shoulder
exiled
or expelled
to us
who welcome them
with warm arms and tears
knowing they would prefer
your icy bosom.

The Grand Gesture

Never the grand gesture
        only the quiet walk
                down a dark alley
I have a talent it seems
        a natural instinct
                a highly developed skill
Never the song
        only the lyrics
                on printed paper
I can do it anywhere
        in the biggest crowd
                in the smallest group
Never the sweeping kiss
        only the wry smile
                on the stone-faced lips
I require no energy
        the heart beats
                the mind turns
Never the high climax
        only the quiet curtain
                on the fading scene
I write
I think
I bleed.

Al

Al
was my mother's brother's name
I don't ever remember meeting him
he died before I was born, or soon after
he was in the war, a soldier
at Guadalcanal or Iwo Jima

he caught no lead there
but later
a time-bomb germ
laid him low
so I would never know
my uncle
Al.

My Father

who gave me five hundred dollars
he didn't have
today
spent this evening
asking about my PhD
and telling me
how to brush my teeth
yesterday he told me
how to drive a car
tomorrow
he may tell me
how to tie my shoes
he loves me
he knows that I am a grown
                educated
                competent man
but
he does not realize
I am no longer
his little boy.

Crescent Moon

Crescent moon
Single star of love
early evening
Sunday before Christmas
Churches hung with poinsettias
    and song
for some kid
born of a knocked-up girl
and a sneaky spirit
dropped into a trough
surrounded by manure
    and oats
so we could chop down trees
sell presents
and get fat
Sing a song of joy.

God of the Lilies

Oh God of the lilies
Who lights like the sun
Who sang such a new song
On a crisp Easter morn
Oh God of the dewdrops
Who cried like a storm
Who died for the children
Yet to be born
Oh God of the hilltops
Who crawled on the ground
Who climbed past the star lanes
With body unbound
We who remain here

And sing you this song
Ask but to follow
On our own Easter morn.

I Have Witnesses

I have witnesses
They have seen it all
The chill stars
Glinting on the pale dogwoods
And the blue lace lilacs
Of another Spring
They have seen it all
The Fall, and Rise
The Time
My not-yet-thirty summers
See only shadows
Leaf green mists
By streetlamps lit
Hints of what was
And Is
Even in my winter
Long past youth
I will not have seen it all
But I have witnesses
And they have seen it all.

For James Dickey

Sitting on a step unit going nowhere
On the theatre loading dock
Watching the red moon
Dying behind the artificial mists
After hearing Big Jim himself
The old night-fighter, Coke ad writer
Summon up a few ghosts
We all find within ourselves
Tuck, the bedtime hunter
And John the Baptist's honey-sweet, severed head
I scribble a few lines myself
Not in imitation, or search of glory
(My search is on a different stage)
But just to say, "Hey, Jim,
Amen!"

Sunrise in My Rearview Mirror

Sunrise in my rearview mirror
Naked mountains cutout against a spectrum sky
Somewhere distant a glowering cloud
      drops life on a mountain
In this old seabed, a cholla grows
A seamless land, pierced by rock ridges
      of earth's crusts
The sun chases me from ridge to ridge
Showing me their shades and colors
The sun is the grand killer here
Everything hides from it
We are in the Dead Mountains
Just south of the Valley of Death
(It's on the map, look it up)
By noon it will be fire here
But God and my Fiat willing
      I will be gone
Over the mountains to the sea
Past the dead and deadly beauty
Of this season of the sun.

Livingston Verses (1980–81)

Understanding Does Not Come

Understanding does not come
From standing on Bourbon Street
A stripper riding a mechanical bull
To small back red-neck woods
        Alabama town
Being hugged and called a sweetie
        and left
Live we in the same world?
Crying nights and sleeping days
An office life with quiet minds
Courage flees the unseen fear
Of gray-haired words backed by
        burning crosses
We drowned in might-have-beens
Breathe the bell jar vacuum of
        our lives
And pray for sins to save our
        mortal souls.

December 8, 1980

Late-night company leaves me wondering
Were parting words an opening
        or a close
Did darkened words belie the
        glitter glance
Shall I call again
On another black and rainy night
Or am I fumbling in the dark
For a touch that isn't there

Far away, a singer died

You wanted to cry, but the newscaster
	thought too much
I wanted to comfort you
But the tears never cried

Don't you understand
I don't know what to do
Call me tomorrow
Drop an explicit hint
I know I am too old to be so young
But I am half Merlin and stand
	twisted in time

How can it be like this
The human race procreates
So not all stare question marks
	into the dark

I don't think too much, honest
I work at it
I just play his songs
But I wonder, at your fading back
How can I sing his songs
	to the empty sky.

Between Reality and Illusion

Between reality and illusion
      lies courage
We know how it is
And, cowards, demand of our illusions
Say it ain't so
And drown by the millstone
      that isn't there
In this warp of time, illusion curves
      back upon reality
Facing our own false front
We see the stranger we never recognize
And only the brave man hides
      his face
The coward says he really isn't there
And you shouldn't show such things
Especially to children and old ladies
Who know better.

Bourbon Street

Have you ever been to Bourbon Street
And seen the dancing girls
And wondered why
I have

I wondered why they danced
Then why we looked
Then I just wondered
Why?

Song for a Friday Afternoon

There's nothing as sad
       as a dream
              come true
Nothing as weak
       as a sigh
Nothing as empty
       as a sleeping place
              with too much room.

The Last Generation

I am having trouble believing anything
Those of us of the Last Generation
Who face despair
About the time I was born
It became possible to kill everybody
In about thirty minutes
We've made it thirty years now
But the strain is beginning to show
Not long after came the silent Spring
Followed by the visible air, and other things
Little men calling themselves giant apes
Hammers and sickles, crescents and stars
Bloody crosses of every kind
Even beliefs that die-hard are killed
So, we grab for all the gusto
Because tomorrow, if there is one
Won't be as good
So you take what you can get
While it's there
And don't believe in anything
Cause that sucker will get us yet.

And Said So

Naked in bed
Reading the comics over her shoulders
(Doonesbury between her breasts)
As ways to begin a Sunday
I could think of worse
Later, slow love and pork chops
Soft thighs and tender loins
Supper by candlelight
Slow slide to tomorrow
On a day I fell in love

And said so.

Morning

I burned my hand
Taking the biscuits
Out of the oven
For the Sunday morning breakfast
After Saturday night love
She was cooking a cheese omelet
I made biscuits and coffee
We were not dressed
I think there will be a small scar
On my hand
Perhaps on my soul as well
For her love is hot
But, despite the danger
It is sometimes good
To warm one's hands
Near a fire.

Let This Be Said

Let this be said
In colder age or silent winter
I have been loved
And did also love
A woman fine and tender
In empty rooms or quiet halls
Mist naked trees or bitter breeze
If all my parchment crumble
For a span of days
In seasons hard or plenty
A woman fine saw me well in her eyes
And wept at the parting after.

Untitled

Beautiful as a metaphor
Shapely as a rhyme
Soft as onomatopoeia
Poetry sans words.

Not Poetic

Desperation is not poetic
When three months out of work
One does not think of "checking account" as iambic
But as a beautiful girl
who vanished at the magician's wave
never to be seen again
Or as a lovely flower
that withered and died
There is no poetry
in an unemployment line
Just bare-light offices
with desk after desk
of unanswered whys
The very air is embarrassed
The counselors avoid your eyes
apologizing for having a job
One does not sing
on the way to the bottom
What lyrics go with moving out
but never moving in
What tune can you hum
while living off compassionate friends
Being unwanted, worthless
has no rhythm or rhyme
Dirges are for the dead
Blues for those alone
Desperation is not poetic
There are no songs
in the unemployment line.

Coach

I live with this cat, see
And on occasions, we hold these deep
      involved, complex, meow-filled conversations
That I never understand a word of
I'm not even sure what I'm saying
Not to mention him
Though usually, I think, he's trying to communicate
      some serious, long-held desire
For cheese, or love, or a good neck scratching
But I'm never sure, so I usually just scratch his back
And though I believe my enunciation
      in cat lingo is rather good
I get the impression he doesn't understand
      every meow I say
The result is usually less than serious failure
      to communicate
Though I guess it could be serious to the cat
      if he wants food
      and only gets his back scratched
My girlfriend occasionally imitates the cat
      when she wants her back scratched
But I suspect there's a bit more
      to that meow too.

Gridiron

It occurs to me
that nothing matters
except maybe football
maybe Alabama is right
and really crucial matters
are decided by linebackers
on lined fields of green
surrounded by a hundred thousand drunks
of one kind or another
those sober in blood
intoxicated by frenzy
or the delirium of a heavy bet
Tell me, Bear
who in felt fedora
walked on water
in posters and in Crimson hearts
Is this all that matters
that your valiant soldiers
win again their crusade
and again for honor and mother, win?
Will those of us who never
tread the numbered field
or cry with passion
for the winning score
never matter in this world
never find the open door
never be counted winners
never know the secret
of coming back

for the winning score?

Puff

I cannot sing
Puff the Magic Dragon
without crying
My eyes crack
my voice tears
After years and times
the effect remains
Childhood lost
brings weeping
But why?
I am not so old
as to foolishly long for youth
or so young
as to fear tomorrow
Other songs
grow old
and die
But Puff
roars yet
in my heart
Do I still long
for Hon-a-lee
or have I never
left it?

After

After making love
I go to wash
and wonder
at the commonness
of it all
a little wiggling
between the legs
of a woman
relieving instinct's drives
done daily by millions
as common as sneezing
neither rare
nor unknown
but kept hidden, secret
to give it mystery
to reserve the illusion
that we are different
when we are not
clouded in power
fogged over by unwritten rules
of culture and propriety
regulated by laws
derived from pre-rubber patriarchs
endangered by disease
and potential bawling responsibilities
we make it more
and less
than it is
it is the gene's drive
to survive
our need to share
and a momentary conquest
of life

in that
there is
no shame
or sin.

Waiting for the Mail

Waiting for the mail
Is like waiting for a new life
       to be born
One is sure something is coming
       sooner or later
But only god, not the poor man waiting,
       controls the time
And while one has some idea what to expect
       at least in outward form and shape
But no sure sign of the
       inner contents
So, postman or stork, are awaited
       nervously, in anticipation
Knowing one's fate, in little way or great,
       will change with the delivery.

Unemployed

It is not good for a man to be thought worthless
Unwanted for any labor of body or mind
Pride does have its value
A writer who is read does not mind begging for bread
But a writer, unread, unknown, unwanted, needs some value
Some scrap of honor to keep soul together

A job is not a job
Not a way to earn a living
It is an affirmation of faith
Someone else believes in you
You are worth something to somebody
You can do something worth paying for
Even if your scraps of paper with nickel words
Are worth less than the blank sheets you typed upon

If no one with money where their mouth is believes in you
To sell a shoe or shuffle a file
Why believe some black ink lines of learned script
Can your future fortune form?

When it counts, there are three or four who will feed me
For a few days at a time
And warm me in a bed with a blanket
(or body, in the case of one)
But a nomad, with suitcase and script in hand
And the writer's unsettling eye and brooding tongue for company
A wanderer since birth, with restless, unsettled ways
Like never expecting to stay in a house long enough to vacuum the
    floor
Is not welcome long, no matter how deep the love or friendship
Those who toil for their daily fare from early light till dusk
Will not long love a scribbler, who, after long lounging

Scratches a few lines a day and calls them diamonds
The Patrons of great times are gone
The artist now studies grantsmanship
Not the weave of textured line
Now the filling out of forms is an art
Even an occupation. Men make livings
Even jobs with pay, of filling out forms
For artists who, finding PhD's and talent worthless
Fight for pennies from heaven DC
Or Good King Ford or BP
Or the Lord High Arts Council
And the artist, many times more learned
And many times more intelligent and creative
Than the MBA, or his secretary
Cannot even get a job filling out forms
Because he has no training or experience
In filling out forms
The irony cannot be forgiven
Cannot even be passed over
Because God is in His Heaven
In whatever justice Heaven brings

Why is it then the poor poet
Who cannot even fill his pockets or his soul
Must (unlike the Filler of Forms, Boss of Lackeys
Banker of Billions, whose cups overflow)
Cry in the emptiness of night
Cry in the hollow of his soul.

Between the Waiting

I should be writing a play
It rests, half done, only pages away
In mid-first draft it lies
      waiting for an ending
But in mid-stride I hesitate
Butting my head against formless tales
Butting my life against formless days
      waiting for a new beginning
I do not have a job or home
In lined notebooks I scribble lines
Instead of unloading and unlimbering electric
      waiting for a place for resting
Waiting are the days, for phone or mail
Watching the nights slide by, unspent
Wandering to a new home in dreams
      waiting for a morning to match them
Plays are hard to write in unsettled times
Placing so many words together wants days
Poetry asks only minutes at a time
      Waiting for the interrupted spaces

Between the waiting.

Consuming Time

Nerves fray
Minds rot
TV, like a drug
Kills the senses
When overused
Abused
Used to deaden time
Time spent waiting
For a reason
Not to wait
Even books
Well written
Must be used
In moderation
Lest tolerance develop
To awe
While consuming time
Eating away life
While waiting
One must, as they say
(So right they are)
Do something
The fragile hours
Spent writing
Cannot support the day
It wants doing
It wants life
Outside the page
Duty done
Job completed
Love fulfilled
Beyond the paper glory
Beyond the silent page.

Have I Loved Thee Well

Have I loved the well
Only to love thee falsely
Only to leave thee well
And not falsely love thee still?
I swear I loved thee
Perhaps again I will
Today my heart is twain
Part for you, part for going
Though I know which you fain
Like welcome shade or cooling rain you were
In my season of scorched, hot weather
But your time is passing and I, a cur
Would seek another home for this long winter
And wait to see if spring and following summer
Bud and bloom your love again to fuller flower.

For Example

What does God want?
Take me, for example, I'm unemployed and living with a girl
My mom says God wants me to learn patience
      to find my mission in life
      to wait till I'm married
My girl says God wants us to stay together
      to learn to relax
      to marry
I just want to get a job
      to get away from my mother
      to get away from my girl
      to get away from here
What does God want?

Kathy, I Swear

Kathy, I swear it was right when it started
I did learn to love you
There were nights, and days, when I did
I was as honest as I have ever been
Had I gone in August, it would have been right
The perfect affair, two honest people
      who for a few months
      loved each other
      and helped each other grow
      become more than we were before
      wiser, braver, a bit more gentle
But I have stayed too long
The honesty is slipping away
The sex is more like a payment
      for services rendered
      not love expressed
You grow used to me, dependent again
      I thought you were past that
I grow restless, uneasy, living another lie
      hiding my soul again
      covering part of my life
      just to have something free
      of my own, not shared
I would go if I could
You know that, I am still that honest
But where, my God, where?

But I'm Leaving

Kathy, I love you
>but I'm leaving

I love the way your bare rump
>rubs my hand while we sleep

I love that wild look you get
>when, well, you know

I love the way you care for me
>out of love more than I understand

But I'm leaving

Not just to find a job
>though my wallet demands

Not just for roads to fame and fortune
>though my calling demands

Not just for freedom or wild oats
>though my innocence demands

But I'm leaving

Because I love you enough
Not to fight your irritating clutter
>of house and time

Not to fight your rigid church
>of rules and forms

Not to fight your loved career
>of service and care

But I love you

Kathy, I'm leaving.

Dear God

Dear God,
Please keep my van safe and sound

For all I own is in it
And I am living in it
Driving from town to town
Searching for the job I've been praying for
    for almost a year
And please keep my parents and friends well
For I visit them for showers and meals
And list their addresses and phone numbers
Counting them as my answering service
Applying for that job I pray to you for
    beginning so long ago
And please keep the economy healthy
For I am running out of money
And would really be in trouble in a recession
Standing in some welfare line
Praying for you to get on the job again
    and answer this prayer.

Fierce Freedom

It's the fierce freedom
I feel, walking alone
nibbling cookies fetched
from a bank contest table
The illusion of the open road
the solitary wanderer
living off the land
independent, his own man
Oh, that calls
Still
I was never that free
No road is really open
and my fate
has never been my own.

Injustice

The fundamental injustice
    in this world
Is that love can give
    birth to sorrow
Can be a fertile field
    for hate
That caring can be
    so pregnant with disaster
Do I, out of fear
    abort my loves
Or, of guilt, carry them to term
    and orphan them
    by leaving
    with their arms
    outstretched to me
Or do I take my first
blind luck for eternity
knowing she will
break my heart.

Titles of Works I Should Write Some Day

"Don't feed me straight lines
    while I'm eating broccoli."

"Whatever happened
    to Tidy Weiderman?"

Saint Mary's Tears

In Nicaragua
they call the rain
Saint Mary's tears
Kathy, I'm crying too
But unlike your tears
which flow into my beard
as I hold you
mine flow inside my cheeks
under my skin
onto this paper
but I am just as sad
at leaving you
and my tears
are just as real
as Saint Mary's tears.

Untitled

Unemployed college professors
brag about the big salaries
they will earn
now that they are out of academia
but they stay unemployed
Old ladies and ugly women
long past the beauty of youth
still struggle with hair
and clothes to "look good"
but never do.

Songbook

In a songbook
borrowed from my sister
I found where she
in her adolescence
had scrawled her name
entwined with some teenage heartthrob
of Hollywood and fame
a new one for each page
sometimes just the name
of some overhyped, young girl's dreamboat
was enshrined alongside the title
of a pop-rock love tune
somehow associated with this lover-boy
but, toward the end,
in a section of almost forgotten oldies
in an innocent, unseeing wisdom
of future, longer days
her name alone was drawn
untied to plastic or electric sweetheart
beside an old, golden Dylan tune
about love being
just a four-letter word.

Atlanta Rain

It is raining in Atlanta
    cold, late February's second winter
I have just bisected the city
    from south of loop to north
Searching for far-flung addresses
    of potential promised lands
Finding half-constructed office complexes
    and slamming-in-face doors

It's like God Himself, despite mercy
    would not grant interviews
Yesterday, in academic Israels,
    I wandered, lost
Speechless and unspoken to
    victim of the Law (EOE/AA)
"To be fair to all
    you must speak to none."
Now I sit in Denny's in Decatur
    watching the rain and waiting
I may have seen one flash of rainbow
    not yet mine, not yet real
But perhaps a promise
    There will be no deluge.

Dream

Did you ever see a dream disappear?
It is not a pretty thing
A cat paws
    at a golden ribbon
Then wonders where it has gone
    when it is jerked away
The cat forgets
    and moves on to other toys
But the dreamer's eyes gleam
    gold and green
Red with held-back tears
    turn white in disbelief
His ribbon was there
    scented with fame
Reeking of glory
    to hungry nostrils
Satin and lace
    to see and touch

The dreamer's hands
      like thumbless paws
Grasp lonely air
      the golden glory
Yanked away
      by an unseen hand
Replaced, perhaps,
      With pale, torn string
It is not a pretty thing.

Future Cold

I wanted to press her flesh into mine
To encircle and engulf her
To keep her there
Warmth against future cold
Later we lay beside
Her head against my chest
Two loves with weeks left only
I was long in finding her
Short in going
I ask not a change of fate
Or more time before parting
Only a love not lost
To time or space
As warmth against future cold.

Troubled

Troubled
Uncertain
Afraid
She gave
herself
to me
Such
Is
Love
Doubting
my love
Scorned
by another
Fearing
her womb
She gave herself
to me
Love
is such
Knowing
I would leave
Wary
of gossip
Seeing
no future
She gave
to me
herself
Such
love
is.

Barbourville Poems (1982–84)

Suddenly Strange

It's strange to sleep alone
After waking up in a woman's room
Watching her dress
And eating her pancakes
With strawberry jam
It's strange to stick out my arm
And touch nothing
After kissing her in the park
Eating a picnic lunch
Chicken, fries, coleslaw
And a soft drink
It's strange how what was familiar
For thirty years
Can be suddenly strange
After so few nights
So few days
Of waking
In a woman's room.

Tanned

The ripe, golden apples of the sun
Shined above her blouse
Ready for plucking and tasting
Like an orchard just before harvest
Full and bountiful
The worms still hidden
Dry, wrinkled age
Still seasons away.

To the Literalists among Us

"Beating a dead horse"
Could mean
Cudgeling the carcass
Of a deceased equine
But it doesn't.

Send Not

I have spent too many afternoons
watching Dan Rather
explain bullet wounds
why should I, a Baptist
have to pray
for a pope
Because I know
those bells
toll for me
as much as any man
Each crazed slug
that strikes flesh
wounds me
with fear
and hate
And even if I
and whichever leader of fame
that falls
live to rise
It is peace
that dies.

A Poem a Day

A poem a day
Keeps the doctor away
I hope
My guts are crying
Two weeks from unemployment
Three thousand dollars from starvation
My insides twist
Playing dodgeball
With fear
And no soft woman
At midnight
Or doctor's little pill
Can massage away
The pain
Below the bones.

The Waste

It seems a waste of time
Spent putting lines on paper
To file away, not unread
Just uncared for, unwanted
Rejected.

Greenwood Lines (1984–87)

Kentucky

The soft, blue mountains
hide such pain
the children clinging
to cloud fleece skirts
tied to her
by ignorance, fear
watching as she is raped
by strangers
fighting brothers, sisters
for the loose change
from the stranger's pockets.

You would not
let me love you.

State of Mississippi

Asshole of America
Ignorance glorified
So prejudiced they hate themselves
Land brown with black and white blood
Closed, out to lunch, forever
Forever afraid, forever poor
Forever Mississippi.

Hospital

From nursery Spring
To winter ICU
And all the Falls and Summers in between
Dr. Chronos carves our lives
Suturing the little cuts

But never staunching the flow
Of lifeblood
As patients come and go
Neonatal unit, hemo lab (Hymen's exam)
Emergency rooms and convalescent wards
Finally the coroner's cold table
From room to room we move
Ward to ward
Always dying
Always living our passing season
In sterile white
And artificial quiet.

In the Shower

Writing poetry
in the shower
is not easy
my habitual pen
is not on me
the only paper in reach
is not for writing on
I must remember a line
as I search for the next
while rubbing my head
with shampoo
remember, edit, create, wash
clean lines and wet hair
fearful some verse
will rinse from my head
and spin, gurgling
down the drain.

Easter

The Easter sun
rises alone
as I lie sleeping
under the electric blanket
Later, I will eat
a plain sandwich
a glass of water
I will not dress
no guest comes
no host would welcome me
to the table
It is quiet
this Easter morn
as I lie sleeping.

If Life

If
life is so wonderful
why
one out of ten thousand suicide each year

If life
is so wonderful
why
do heroin needles ever go in arms

If life is
so wonderful
why
alcohol, cocaine, and angel dust

If life is so
wonderful
why
Hare Krishna, Moon, or Jim Jones
why
ulcers, angina, or hypertension
why
terrorists, rebellions, or wars

If life is so wonderful
why?

Dirty Poem

I would like to write a dirty poem
About slipping cocks into cunts
While sucking tits
And feeling up pussies
While getting my dick sucked
A poem that would get penises hard
While making vaginas sopping wet
So that everyone who reads it
Would have to run out and fuck somebody
Or at least jerk off alone
But everybody would cum
Simultaneously orgasming
Bursting with sexual pleasure
Simmering in genital heat
That is the kind of poem
      I would like to write
But if I did
My mother would kill me.

Walls

Breaking down walls
I can say fuck now
At least in its literal use
At least to a select few
My darns have become damns
I understand the irony in my name
I know I am not handsome
Or rich
Or great
Certainly not popular
Or right
All the time
I am a very quiet
Socially maladjusted
Highly organized
Intelligent
Educated
Loner
Hitting middle age
After missing childhood
And youth
Wondering if I will quietly die
Somehow endure
Or someday explode.

Cubicle

As I sit in my cubicle
Listening to the un-windowed wind blow
Listening to the babble of the other teachers
      in nearby classrooms
Wondering what the weather is becoming
I dream of doing great deeds

Writing great plays, saving the world
        or at least some wonderful women
Who thank me by sharing their bodies
With long, slow sex
Mini-orgies, two or three at a time
Love with no limits
A sharing of a man too great
        for just one woman
We lick and suck, screw and fuck
Because of the love and care
        for the wonder that is me
Who is sitting in his cubicle
Listening to the hidden wind.

Mental Locomotive

I have got to get out of here
Searching for the secret shores
Cathouse love, here pussy, pussy
What vaginal lips these lips have kissed
        and where and why
These people don't like to hear the truth
Horny, wet women call me
        But never come
Assholes of America, unite
You have nothing to lose but your cherry
I regret that I have but one cunt
        to fuck for my country
Call me cocky, but let me come.

Border

On the border
Between living
And existing
I stand
On the edge
On the ledge
Looking up
Looking in
Feeling tremors
In the ground
Fault sounds
Shifting fields
Magma rising
Eruptions coming
To lift me
To a higher mountain
Or drop me
In collapsed land.

The Only Time

The only time sex is important
Is when you aren't getting any
There's no fucking justice
In a world with no fucking
Something everybody needs
Something everybody wants
Something everybody can give
The perfect present
Suitable for all occasions
Yet hidden, saved, rationed
As if it improves with age
Screwing is not a wine

In limited supply
The shortage is artificial
There's a social embargo
A government ban
An outdated command
A false fear
Conditioned paranoia
That's killing people
Starving the weak
The halt, the lame
The social cripple
Wasting away
With a lonely hand.

Dying on the Vine

Killing time and brain cells
with cabled-in electric poison
hiding in my room
pretending to be an island
dried-up pens scattered about
dusty manuscripts and bland pages
white walls, no pictures
a well-padded cell
crosswords and silence
canned tuna and instant rice
I should, I should, I should
but pain, too much pain
inside, outside, demons or fools
old songs to hold me
Something terribly wrong with me
Shriveling, past ripe
The Time long gone.

Back to Roots

Back to roots, to basics
I breathe, I eat, I sleep
I write?
I need air, food, warmth
Love?
So how?
Air, free
Food, bought
Shelter, rented
That leaves
Never free
Not for sale
Not for lease
Must be earned
Or given
Can't force giving
Leaves earning
How?
Live, love, laugh
Laughter bites
Live, love
Life hurts
Love
Who, what?
Any?
Fools?
Maybe
Enemies?
Sure
And get?
Ignorant hate
Just great
Sorry

So?
No answer
No answer?
No answer
Just great.

The Sound

The Sound! The Sound!
The Silence
Sounds in my ears
Drowns out thought
The throbbing quiet
Pounds my mind
An unheard scream echoes
Screeching, deafening
Ripping sanity
Crashing saneness
To tinkling bits
Trumpeted away
In the howling wind
Of silence.

Not a Factor

Time is not a factor
To the mind
The body ages slow/fast
The mind stays young/old
The dreams fresh/stale
We hit the wall
At different times
Some old at ten
Others grow young again
Just suddenly comes when
And then.

Undark Night

Walking the undark night
So many lights
Porch, car, window, street
Stars are only in planetariums
And the sounds
Engines, horns, TV, doors
Crickets are in zoos
So this is modern life
Forever lonely
Never alone.

Comparisons

Why can't I write like e.e.
But with capitals
Or solitary Emily
But without rhyme
Sing like Bonnie Bobby
But in American
Sound like Big Jim
But less macho
How did they get free
And not me?

The Same Poem

I am tired of writing the same poem
Over and over again
Only the names and dates are changed
Monday is Saturday is Wednesday is
No difference
Hell is eternity

Tomorrow and tomorrow and tomorrow
Another today, another yesterday
Another another
Another again.

The Blues

A raw emotion
Refined, distilled, crystalized
Into sparking joy.

Rock

The rock has cracked
Wind and tide wait no more
Wearing the shards to
Smooth, pointless pebbles.

The Tree

One wildness stood solitary
Near a corner of cultivated ground
Prematurely bald
Under the high sun burning
Stripped and twisted by flatland wind
White with age, being worn away
By nature's man-unleashed hand.

I Have Spent

I have spent
So much time
Not loving
And not allowing
Myself to be loved
That only
The fear
Of losing
Your love
Stops me
From taking
Love
From others.

I Never Had a Chance

I never had a chance
No choice was good
No choice was mine
One way sorrow
One way fear
No way open
No way near
Cry, sigh, or die
Face loneliness
Poverty, or tears
Flip the coin
Roll the die
Pay the dealer
The house always wins
You can't go home again
Not from this crap-shoot
This dunghill of life

Where living ain't easy
We're covered in sixes
So nobody wins
There aren't any odds
Nothing comes out even
When the dealer is
An unsmiling God.

Broken Heart

A broken heart
Beats differently
And often stops
Exhausted
By adrenaline highs
That never came down
Burned out on no's
OD'ed on dreams denied
It dies
No wonder why.

Dismember

There's not a heck of a lot left
When they dismember you
From the inside out
Gulping your manhood
Burning out your guts
Slicing your heart to slivers
And sucking the blood
Draining life from the shell
That is all that's left
Of me.

My Night

My night
is like some winded watches
raged through
by sailors in some
North Atlantic blow
tossed as if by waves
o'er breaking bow
turned by roaring currents
racing round.

That I Try

I want to explain
What you cannot understand
Any more than I can understand
A woman's monthly change
Or womb's yearning for a child
You will not understand
But it is a sign
Of how deep my love is
That I try
I have been alone
Terrifyingly alone
For a God's age
In an isolation
Beyond imagining
Deep in fear
And hate
Cut off from humanity
By my own shattered soul
And a child's fate
Of cruel, mindless torture
Sent by some avenging deity

I grew up alone
Knowing no other survival
No other way
Watching flowers grow
In a garden
I lived outside
A wild flower
Trodden underfoot
Unaccepted
Among the blooms

How alone can a man be
I can sing that song
The soul that has never been open
The tune that is never played
I have secrets you will never know
Poems you will never hear
Listen to me
I never loved
Until you loved me
Was never warm
Until you held me
Was never known
Until you knew me
You made me feel
Gave me freedom
And I loved you
Love you

I am trying to bloom now
Trying to heal my shattered soul
Become a man
Find my sight
In the blinding light
Do not fear if I

Bend to touch another flower
Now that I have joined the garden
Nor cry if my leaves
Touch another rose
My roots are deep in your soil
Rooted in the life you gave me
But, like the hawk
Which soars above
I am only truly yours
When you set me free
Your tether may hold me
But not my spirit
When I can soar
Mayhaps to other hands
But return to you
Unleashed
Then we are both free
And bound by a stronger cord
Some things you cannot have
Totally
But must share
Though it breaks your heart

I am not hawk
Or flower
Only alone
And breaking
On the rocks
Of the rough coast
Needing many small harbors
On this long voyage
Your deep port
Is safe harbor
But I have been shut up
In dry dock

Too many years
I need the sea
And its storms
But you must be there waiting
My safe harbor
Service other boats
If you will
But do not condemn me
To your inlet
On pain of banishment
If I sail beyond the bar

Cry for me
You weep for yourself
When isolation visits
He lives with me
Your loins ache
Yet you are seldom long between lovers
I am years alone
The pain is permanent
Aside from you
I can count my wild nights
On my fingers
You have never been alone
Not truly alone
Not staring God in the eye alone
You have no Christmas sobbing on your knees alone
No hospital ceiling blank nights alone
Which friend will you call tonight
Which well-known heart will beat for you
Which well-worn ear share your secrets
My phone has no dial
I leave "Permanent Address" forms blank
And always have

So I sit here
Alone
You are far away
A memory
A voice on the phone
I weep for me
Alone
Those here who would comfort me
Cannot
For I cannot touch them
You say I cannot
Or I lose you
My job says I cannot
Or I lose my career
My mind says I cannot
Or I lose my control
So I do not
And lose my stomach
Or my mind
Or my soul
And they grow away from me
As I turn away from the sea

Fate is not kind
Life is short
Youth a sprinter
Tell me
Is there no room for joy
Are there no little loves
Must care for one hurt another
Can I write but not live
You love me
And fear to lose me
I love you
And fear to lose you

Why are we so unhappy
Is faithfulness so important
That happiness is its price
Are man and woman so different
We can never understand
I am coming to pieces
Like burned and broken cobblestone
I fear the night
And each little ache or pain
Like age or death
Have I lived
Is there no way to love
I am confused
Unsure
And alone
My life hangs by puppet strings
Pulled by an unknown master
Who may not like me
Is there no comfort here
Why is love such a sin
It does no good to cry
Nor is there room to complain
Without blasphemy
Can you not love me
Despite the time
Is there no consolation
No balm in Gilead
No empathy for man
Alone
In a world of fire
And burning
Will passion crack the ice
Or will you find my yours
Alone

And cold
And you unable to understand

The Hindus (or the Chinese)
Used to believe that a man
Could gain strength
By being inside a woman
And give back that strength
To the woman
In who he came
So they would have sex
Without orgasm
With ten women a night
Gathering strength
For that one most favored woman
To whom they gave their life
I think
In my insane moments
That love is like that
The more love we share
With others
The more we have to give
To that special one
Yet you must think otherwise
Believing that my love will build
If kept to you yourself
Cut off from all others
Fearing it is limited
And can be stolen
One of us
I suppose, is wise
But I do not know
Which one

So, I near the end

Or a beginning
Or a transition
Knowing I love you
Knowing I am alone
Knowing you will never understand
Not knowing where I am going
How the flower will grow
How the hawk will soar
Or where the road will turn
Only knowing
I am alone.

Imagine

I want you to imagine something
Imagine
That for six years
After you left college
No man touched you
Loved you
Cared for you
In that six years
You moved four times
Over four hundred miles each time
Without any aid
To unknown places
Never seen before
In those six years
People came to your home
Six times
You broke bread at other tables
Twice
You phoned a friend to talk
Never
In those six years

You developed an ulcer
Went into therapy
Had no pets
Only got home for Christmas
Four times
In those six years
You never loved
Were never loved
Never kissed
Never touched

Then
Imagine
When all seems lost
A man
Welcomes you into his life
Into his bed
Into his love
For a year
Then is gone

Can you imagine?
You who never lived alone
Until yesterday
Whose phone calls to friends
Cost hundreds
Who has spent so many nights
In the arms of men
Who likes to go home
To parents and childhood friends
Who has a dog or cat
In even the loneliest hours
Can you imagine?

Now imagine

The beloved is far away
The future uncertain
Life unsure
But by some miracle
Another man (or men)
Is perhaps willing
To share your odd night
To share a few moments
Of warmth
Knowing there is nothing more
But a moment's comfort
But he, and all the others
Are forbidden
By law
By morality
By the beloved's fear
But the beloved is far away
The nights are cold
There is no one
To talk to
Not even of little things
Can you imagine?
Is it any wonder
My soul twists
In torment

Can you imagine?
Can you imagine?

Both Ways

You can't have it both ways
Expecting me to love you
But not be attracted
To those who share your spirit
Love is not a faucet
To turn on or off
At will
It is a brook
That runs
Or dries.

Roses

Fireworks are roses
Black-stemmed in the sky
Sitting on the road bank
Before the Fourth of July
Watching the firelights
Shimmer and die
Wondering why liberty went
To the great bye and bye
Leaving songs and illusions
Red rockets and pie
Flame-breathing flowers
Delusions of time
For we're shackled by commerce
Imprisoned by rhyme
Gold bars and green paper
Tie down our mind
Till we pay for our prison
Enslaved in a line
By illusions of flowers
Of freedom, of time

Of roses a-burning
Dimming our minds.

Villanelle

Like sounds of hearts known never
      Passed over amid the throng
Such silence should be shunned forever

The lone, the flower plain, but clever
      Who sits by walls of song
Like sounds of hearts known never

The odd man out will one day sever
      A life that ends in endless wrong
Such silence should be shunned forever

So quiet, they say, a loner, why whoever
      Would have believed; an evensong
Like sounds of hearts known never

So passes pain, a life uncried, an endeavor
      Failed, a song that never could belong
Such silence should be shunned forever

And who shall sing, say I, and whatever
      Is my song is sad and long
Like sound of hearts known never
Such silence should be shunned forever.

Villanelle 2

Like little girls dancing naked in a stream
        Little joys of childhood disappear
Like little boys running barefoot in a dream

Innocence is not all it may seem
        But visions of it oftentimes appear
Like little girls dancing naked in a stream

To surprise our eye, a bit of youth redeem
        Both more and less, regret and fear
Like little boys running barefoot in a dream

I would not go back, crave candy and ice cream
        But rather wish such joy was near
Like little girls dancing naked in a stream

Big boys dream of girls' limbs that gleam
        Big girls of brazen men, the modern buccaneers
Like little boys, running barefoot in a dream

So time steals, none dance or dream
        And soon forget the memory clear
Of little girls dancing naked in a stream
Of little boys running barefoot in a dream.

Villanelle 3

A soul left alone to find his way
      A man gone cold in silence ice
For this there will be hell to pay

There is nothing as twisted, as hates the day
      Nothing for which there is a higher price
As a soul left alone to find his way

Someone sans softness, no word to say
      No memory of tender, no knowledge of nice
For this, there will be hell to pay

Who do we blame, guilt at what feet lay
      When all passed by, not thinking twice
A soul left alone to find his way

To you, I say, who would not stay
      Who gifts of love considered vice
For this there will be hell to pay

There will be blood, in time there may
      Be tears, as to him are passed God's dice
A soul left alone to find his way
For this there will be hell to pay.

July 4, 1985, Atlanta

Morning street lined with wives, children, friends
cheering the tailenders
who jog and smile and wave
running for T-shirts and joy

Afternoon we stand above the raining street
sheltered by parking garage level four
and are attacked by thousands of red balloons
loosed to signal the parade
the wind whips the balloons under our roof
as we scamper and laugh for joy

Evening waiting, waiting in rain for dark
to blaze the sky with fire and flame
under the umbrella we wow and ah
red, green, yellow, blue showers overhead
spins, wheels, bursts, burns, and falls
changing to water that splashes at our feet
changing thunder and lightning into bolts of joy.

Fireworks

To turn dark night to glory you must employ
  Not searching lights but childhood's rockets
The fire and flame of freedom's joy

Blue sparklers, pen wheels, a blazing grownup toy
  This, not trinkets, gold beads, or silver lockets
To turn dark night to glory you must employ

Such light shines not from uniformed, bemedaled viceroy
  For this bright burst you must put on the docket
The fire and flame of freedom's joy

And monochrome quiet is just a false decay
        Rejected by sons of Bowies and Crocketts
To turn dark night to glory you must employ

The shifting, whirling, dazzling flash all men enjoy
        The soaring, falling, bursting, blasting sky-rocket
The fire and flame of freedom's joy

A pox on those who would purify the alloy
        Or tie the flare to some silent socket
To turn dark night to glory you must employ
The fire and flame of freedom's joy.

Bloody Haiku

Punch drunk, staggering
        The fighter claws toward corner
                Hoping he hears bells.

Scar Tissue

Scar tissue
Does not feel
Nerves that screamed
Do not regenerate
So each little cut
Or big cut
Or great cut
To the heart
Reduces me
To unfeeling.

Little Tragedies

Little tragedies produced but unreviewed
The wails heard only by the broken soul
Our lives play tearfully to empty houses

There is silence in the wings
As we fret our hour on the stage
Without prompt or stage directions

Only the ghost of the boards
Sees our all-too-common show
Hears our oft-echoed lines in silence

There will be no applause, no bow
When rings the curtain down
We took our role as cast

Remembered our lines, hit our marks
And made our exits
Without bumping into the furniture

Alas, poor Yorick, no one knew him well
Soliloquies and monologues
We are such stuff, till only pages

Are left, yellowing, turning to dust
Lost manuscripts
Of ill-remembered plays.

The Ring

I have a diamond engagement ring
Hidden away in a briefcase
Among insurance papers and old letters

Gathering dust and losing luster
In the darkness
She said I should trade it in
Perhaps on a VCR
But I put it in its box
And stored it away
Like hope hiding in a drawer.

April, Mississippi

Green Spring
hippity heat
soul-searing sun
Ford sauna
melting across wet asphalt
riding rails over shrunken rivers
(no starch, please)
let it hang limp
hair does today
tongues too
panting steam
no A/C in poverty/outdoors
just sweat
a season ahead of the calendar
Delta down here
digging, dying
rotting unborn
cotton wet and dry
wait until July
then it really gets hot.

In the *New Yorker*

In the *New Yorker* poetry of mine
just will not fit. No such sophisticate
am I. I'm just a Southern boy, unversed
in city life, so very unrehearsed
for talk o're teacups bone and delicate,
for references to artists Florentine.
So too for Poetry, the holy shrine
of densest verse, that claims to hold the state
of printing best in form and thought, so first
the poet's reputation comes, who nursed
the rhymes till thirst and mind the lines do sate.
I'm hungry still, but pen will not resign.

The Sprinter

My feet are latex
Near naked I stand
         and kneel
         and fly
    at the flash of the shot
trying to touch the golden strand
     before the sound has died.

Whenever the Morning Newspaper

Whenever the morning newspaper
Is not on the lawn
I wonder if the world is ending
And the reporters found out
And went home
Rather than bannering the news
Like a cartoon prophet

Leaving the rest of us
To face the end
Unknowing
Over cereal or donuts.

I Sometimes Wonder

I sometimes wonder
why we consider
the soft, virgin snowfall
a symbol
of innocence and purity
when each white snowflake
requires a sooty speck of sin
about which to crystalize
its life.

There's a Difference

There's a difference between
The way old lovers touch
And the eager new
There's no exploring
They know
How to cup the hand
To fit the breast
As natural as a football
In a wide receiver's soft hands
As welcome as old friends
On a Sunday afternoon.

Proposal to Kathy

Consider me
A la Al Jolson
On my knee
Singing I love you
Singing the song
I never sang
To one girl before
Let me sing

Come, woman of joy
Be my wife
Let us burn our passions together
Till time makes us old friends
Who warm each other's lives
As the world grows cold

Let me sing your glory
Let me lie in your arms
     when you laugh
Let me hold you in my arms
     when you cry
Let me lie down beside you
     in the dark lonely night
Let me dance with you
     in the bright shining day
Let us eat together
     the chocolate candy happiness
Let us drink together
     the castor oil pain
Let us give birth to flowers

Let us buy a five-dollar license
That comes with no guarantees

Only promises
I promise you
That love will grow
Will ebb and flow
That we, and life, will change
Life is change
Alone or together
God grant we ride the wave of time
Together

God did not promise me tomorrow
Nor grant me second sight
I can guarantee nothing
But today's love
But if my little wisdom
Tells me anything
It is that
I want you
    near me
    beside me
    touching me
    singing me
    loving me
And I you
And that will be good
    and bad
Easy, and hard
Spring, and Winter

I am wise enough to know
I know little
I know this
I want
Like a guitar wants music
Or paper, words

For us
To be friends and lovers
To touch and to cling
In light and in dark
In sorrow and in joy
In glory and in shame
In heyday and in disaster
In boredom and in delight
In ecstasy and in pain
To give gladly body and mind
To respect and trust
To merge our lives into a single stream
Flowing through the hills and valleys of life
As long as the grass grows
And the rivers run

Send me your song
Send me your dance
Send me your yes.

Doraville Dances (1987–2003)

The Wind Is Singing

Outside my thermo-pane
double-glass, insolated window
the wind is singing
I can tell because
the tree limbs are keeping time
the tune is unheard
beneath the rush
of air conditioner fan
the roar of I-285 traffic
the thunder of planes headed for Hartsfield
and the beep of a backing truck
this mechanized chamber group
does not play Brahms
or even Ives
no wonder then
the waterfall has fallen
out of modern music
no brook babbles on the radio
Windsong is a perfume
not a top-forty tune
we sing what we hear
we do not hear
the melody of leaves.

I-285, Seven a.m.

The red/white snake
scraped across dawn
doing sixty, sixty-five, more
in a loop
those on her back
rode the ride
slowly poisoned each other

or bit with metal fangs
then circled back
each evening
(when the stripes reversed)
and ended up
going nowhere.

Dreams

Why do we dream
of high school sweethearts
twenty years unseen
untraced through time
is it ripe youth we seek
as the sap slows in our veins
or plain purity
the girl untouched
or the mystery of passage
where are we now
converge, diverge
lines met at a point
a non-Euclidian world
warped space-time
has curved us to where
a two-body, four-space
quantum dynamics lost love equation
is unsolvable by ordinary calculus
so night dreams
show Pegasus flying
into gray mists
while my down-to-earth wife
slumbers snoringly beside
Dreams are what you can't have
what never was, never will be
and those are the dreams
that never let me be.

You Can't

You can't write about silence
it doesn't move
it has no color
your own screams cannot break it
it stands
like a prison guard on watch
it burns
like an ulcer, slow and steady
you can't even listen for it
it creeps
like fog on a black night
it stings
like a thousand fleas
you can't even die from it
and that becomes your greatest fear
that it will follow you beyond the grave.

Tammy and Jim

Tammy and Jim
it's such a surprise
to learn you're a doper
and a screwer of men
We'd never have guessed
though Amiee Simple knew
away in Mexico
with you know who
And Minister Billy Jim
(remember him?)
who said the vows
for those he knew
(biblically, both women and men)
suspected at least

But they're forgotten
since never TV'ed
so we're surprised
by pills and whores
But the sin is ours
for forgetting the past
for accepting words
for believing in men.

I've Been Lost

I've been lost
Like a caller put on hold
Accidentally disconnected
Singing Simon's America Tune
Second verse
"I don't have a friend..."
"I don't know a dream..."
The browning leaves of summer
Fallen too soon
Before their time
Before their life
To die without their autumn glory
Lost, uncheered
A blaze of scarlet
Too soon lost.

The Crystal Thought

There is virtue in simplicity
The diamond is not complex
only pure
The crystal thought
or sparkling image
Outshines the multi-strata stone.

No More Time

There's no more time for the green songs
sung by the woodfire cold and gray
for the glories of the green hill
now red and brown. Life falls away.
No more time for the Indian wind
of chilling cheeks and crystal skies
for cricket tunes or fresh-made pies
not from a can. Life falls away.

And in our rush to coldness, o're crackling leaves
dropped dead before us, past greener
passion times when sap ran strong
let once again the breeze strum
our stiffened limbs in one more
warm wild song, before life falls away.

The Pin-up

What were you thinking
When you posed
With hands on hips
Bathing suit pulled down
Below your breasts
Were you thinking of the money
Or how good it was to be beautiful
Or how sexy it felt to reveal yourself
Or of the hot lights and stiff muscles
Or that you were not a person
Only a picture
Did you think of young boys
And lonely old men
Playing with themselves
As they stared at your image

And did that please you
Did you ever think of me
Sitting at my desk
Wondering who you are
Where you come from
Why you did it
What you were thinking
When you posed?

Employee 309

Employee 309
interfaces CRT 154
to edit Doc. ID #2084
(password DAD)
silently wishing some #2
would be deposited
on Adm. #9.

A Bathroom Stall

A bathroom stall
is one place
you can just
sit and think
and no one
will ask you
what you're doing.

First Anniversary

The first is paper, so they say
Easy to tear and throw away
No great cost to those still poor
A card or flowers from the store

But on this, our year today
I am torn over what to say
The cost is great, behind the door
In tears, in fears, as troubles pour

Dreams to nightmares turned
The hopes that year-long burned
Are leaving ashes on the tongue
Naive love songs hurt when sung

We knew it would not be easily done
That white day of rain and sun
It has been beyond imagining
As bad as worst-case planning

The moves, the unemployment lines
The long, unbroken separate times
The doctors, soreness, and the pain
Unsaid words, silent rhymes, touch abstain

So I stand, 365 days past "I do"
The starving poet too close to true
With more fingers than dollars to summon
Far from silver, gold, or diamond

What can I give then but words, to say
Had I known that day this day

I would again take your hand
And firmly beside you stand

If another year, or ten, or twenty on
Bring no better, no brighter dawn
I would again take your hand
And firmly beside you stand

For love is love is love
When old push come to old shove
I want your breast to dry my eye
Your voice to call me nigh

So here I stand, full heart, empty hand
Knowing this is less than planned
Hoping the shining days still shine
Amid clouds and rain and numbing grind

Praying, even with a year of time
You, in love would accept rhyme
And would again take my hand
And firmly beside me stand.

Dec. 1974

I remember boy/man
In desert not home
One 24th eve
As night crept in
The promised love not appearing
By post or parcel service
Dark, business day done
The morning loomed empty
Cursing fates and tardy fathers
He did his vacant chores
Ate blank food
Faced the achingly cheerful TV
And prepared, in the one-room
    basement garret ($90/mo, utilities paid)
To sleep late
And not complain
During call to mother/father/sister
On the morrow
Suddenly the hasty steps
The quick knock
And faster retreat
He opened the door
No one
Then
Below
On the step
A box
Was it?
Some late-night UPS Santa
He pulled it in
Tore it open
Inside, boxes
In colored paper
And ribbons

He sat
And cried
Then placed the presents
On his desk
He did not open them
That was for the morning
To share the time
With those afar
It was enough
Tonight
To know
And so, with true prayers
He went to gentle sleep.

Anniversary II

Two years and counting
and loving
Now
it is hard to sleep
without your breast in my hand
Now
it is difficult to eat
without your voice in my ear
Now
it is impossible to joy
without your love in my heart
Now
let two become twenty times two
let time stir, seasons trade one for another
let us ride the wave of change together
for you are my home, my comfort
for you are my delight, my thrill
for you are my wife
Now
and ever will.

Haiku 3

From five little sounds
Followed by seven and five
A thought leaps and dies

Haiku, you coo too
A dove, white wings, quick, calm, here
Good for city life

The quiet raindrop
Dropping from sky to hard roof
Is silent till end.

Women

Women
become obsessed
about thirty-five
with giving birth
tick tock
La Leche
Someone to come home to
They want "a baby"
Like it would stay that way
forever
never become
        a brat   a patient an expense
        a druggie   an easy lay   a whore
        a lost cause   a false hope   a failure
        a problem   a broken heart   a criminal
Like it never
        makes you cry   drives you up a wall
        wears you out   takes your dreams
        ruins your life   leaves you

Like lemmings
they are driven
to the birthing room
and dare you not
stand in their way.

Season of the Soul

Winter trees
Rip eyes
Like Velcro
Bleeding tears
Down scared cheeks
Winter winds
Bite holes
Like chisels
Spurting blackness
From wrinkled lips
Giving birth
Is the Ultimate Cruelty
Spring should not
Come again.

She Wants

She wants
> to go to Spain
> to drive out west
> to have a baby
> to dress well
> to not work
> to be thin
> to sleep more
> to be popular
> to be married
> to have a family
> to live happily
> to eat out
> to have a house husband
> to have a maid
> to make everybody happy
> to have a nice house
> to eat ice cream
> to ignore time
> to do her job well
> to retire early
> to have money
> to have children

It never seems to occur to her
that some wants
are mutually
exclusive.

Fast Food

If Ronald McDonald
clown that he is
married Mrs. Winner
for her coleslaw
would they have
little baby chicken burgers
or would it be a sterile marriage
because of fat in the tubes?
Or if Colonel Sanders
the old lecher
seduced young Wendy
with his large-size fries
would she bear him
seven secret herbs and spices
then demand child support
or wrap them in a sesame seed bun
and carry them home?

The Gate

My father is a gate guard now, he works
outside a mill. His post a shack of brick
and glass inside a wire fence. It irks
me sore to know his twilight tears some trick
of fate has set. I see him yet in times
gone by, in Sunday shoes, in coat and tie,
in pulpit standing, Bible by, with rhymes
and verses preaching, teaching, all a sigh
o're sins and follies mortal, of men and grace,
of God on high, of faith and Jesus Christ.
He wore God's glory then, it filled the space
around his feet of clay. It's gone, a heist
of time. A fallen soul remains within the wall
to guard a lower gate, await a higher call.

Challenger

Seven ashes to four winds
to scattered bodies go
Roger, throttle up
104 percent of max
and then, beyond
scattered ashes go
The Face of God
fills the screens
Roger, throttle up
beyond the max
Houston, do you copy?
the stars have changed
Do you copy, Houston?
it's a new sky
Houston, do you copy?
All systems go at throttle up
Roger, Challenger
This is Gus at CapCom
You're go for high orbit
Gus?
Yeah?
Hell of a ride
Roger that
Roger, go for high orbit
Throttle up.

The Maya

The Maya
who ripped the beating heart
from the chest of the human sacrifice
thought
he was pleasing God

The Inquisitor
who thrust the burning iron
into the flesh of the heretic
thought
he was defending God's Word

The Pharisee
who paid the crowd
to cry "Crucify, Crucify!"
thought
he was saving God's Nation

I fear
somewhere
another holy man
is thinking.

When Writing

When writing poetry
always double space
between the lines
It's a clue
as to where
the real poetry
lies.

Word Games

Playing word games
All that's left seems
Stealing old lines
Sliding downtimes
I'll forget names
Old wet moon dreams
Null, void, gone rhymes.

Rhymes

Rhymes
twist words
in rhythms
iamb, trochee
pentameter and
various and sundry
convoluted artifice
combinations fabricated
by formalized, villanelled cortex
unaware of alternate synapses.

e.e. hoppergrass

e.e. hoppergrass
far and wee
liberated me
from to be
      or not
but who
from me
will free
the see?

My Wife

My wife wants a baby
I'm not so sure that's wise
    My options are
A.   shut up and fuck
B.   divorce her
C.   have a secret vasectomy
I need a D.

The Weeds

The weeds by the road
      are blooming purple
These in the fallow field
      are yellow
The grass
      is very green
There should be a Romantic poem
      in here somewhere
But Wordsworth
      is dead
And I'm a
      Selective Realist.

To Say I Love

How many ways
to say I love
with words of course
gentle touch, sex
the glance or gift
poem, child, home
time, concern, care
kiss, caress, calm
tears, years
till no question
no doubt
just knowing
eases the long night.

It May Be Time

It may be time to call a halt
to say so long one more time
to stroll on down the mall
to shop another store
A song from Muzak sets the tune
to window shop and wander
to avoid the hassles and the debts
to never show your Visa
You never owe favors, never need friends
so safely pass the door revolving
so sail you home sans baggage
to stop at closing empty armed
And never have belongings.

A Red, Red Nose

My love has a red, red nose
that's newly wiped in June
My love's like Motley Crew
who sweetly play kazoo
So fart thee well my only love
so deep in shit am I
And I will love thee well my dear
till all the still goes dry
Till all the still goes dry my dear
and my rocks ache for your bum
And I will love your cunt my dear
while the juice of life shall come.

Test

I see skulls
in the flower print
of the bedspread
and wonder
if the anonymous artist
deliberately concealed
death heads
in the greenery
as some macabre joke
on unwary sleepers
or if it's me
my unique perspective
of inkblots or daises
that stares back at me
through empty sockets
a mirror
of my mind.

What Women Want

What women want us for
is to get them pregnant
the rest is window dressing
just give them a baby
maybe keep the tigers away
they use us
then let us die
our early deaths
drained and spent.

Old Pain

If I have a child
who at age nine
meets my old pain
how do I look them in the eye
how do I tell them why
do I lie and say
life is wonderful anyway
do I run and hide
compounding pain with shame
Your mother wanted a baby
We didn't think you'd . . .
I'm sorry
I know it hurts
I know.

12th Floor

12th floor, glass-walled
befogged, becalmed
ship of enterprise, (private)
sits airy bemisted
tree green land/sea below
other high-rise masts
hazy to starboard
awash in capitalism
asea in cloud
in my mind
a foghorn sounds.

Sideways

Don't	read	it	period	period	period
read	it	should	at	sideways	like
this	top	be	least	poems	down
poem	to	more	will	go	side
left	bottom	right	make	strangely	up
to	please	that	sense	like	cake
right	period	way	then	that	period

Gunfighter

It is true, when the wind was strong
I sailed on fear, and rode on song
The days, like ages, rolled
The slowest hand, the longest soul

Then time, and a bullet in the spine
Left the legs limp, the hands blind
The clear eyes to the window rolled
See the sea, and regret the goal.

H. R. W.

Letters to her father
you lived well
and died easy
the kid across the street
mourned beside the old man
you went to school with
and your daughter cries
proud she brought you home
to die inside the frame and joint
your hands made, and loved
proud of her old man
who could fix anything
except dying
proud she was there
through all the living
proud of you
and not regretting
your new, deathless joy
but missing you
and not forgetting
there is no good-bye
only *vaya con dios*
see you later
alligator.

9/9/89

toward the last
when the mind thought
the sodden limbs
were chained
you remembered
exactly where

the crowbar was
left corner of the garage
behind the trash cans
but none of your beloved tools
lined so carefully
along the workshop wall
could break these bonds
age, cancer, pressured heart
and the two women
who cared for you
could only laugh
eighty-two
too weak to move
wanting a crowbar
to pry off death.

Dead Yet

"Am I dead yet?"
The old man asked
In sane delirium
"Did the cancer get me?"
No regret
Just curiosity
"Have the funeral notices gone out?"
Inhabiting another world
He faced reality

The doctor
Unprepared for such eternity
Had no answer.

In 1989

In 1989
we dined
on peppermint
and lemon rind
beautiful flowers
surrounded the bier
cold hands
hot tears
applause, applause
and layoff blues
listen to the news
it was a year
of scars
a slice in the cornea
that clears
the eye
to see
and fear
the years.

Squirrels

drink from the birdbath
and eat the sunflower seeds
the birds drop
from the feeder
they hide nuts
among the leaves
and shiver
when the breeze
foretells the time to come
they climb the tree
fold their little paws

and chatter
to the squirrel god
praying
for mild winds
and clumsy birds

And from my own
square, wooden nest
I watch the leaves fall
consider fire and ice
and whisper
Amen.

Lights

The first lights
were clear, hard
bright filaments
glaring in the night
civilization grew
a diffuse coating
was spread inside
softening the beam
now new tints appear
many modern colors
to shade the light
so each can see
truth colored
to his view.

Forgotten Dreams

A bare lightbulb
a table
no cloth
one chair
maybe a cot
or thin mattress
on the floor
one window
closed
barred
no curtain
solid door
deadbolt
chain
Twelve-inch TV
black and white
rent to own
one blanket
two shirts
two shoes
a pair of jeans
a spoon
a can of beans
to eat
like
forgotten dreams.

The Congregation

The congregation
of mourning doves
on the birdbath
make their absolution

sip the sacramental pool
and wing to heaven
like prayers of fools.

The Cat

The cat
covers his eyes
with his paw
to sleep

the world
is much too bright
for his peace
and quiet

and I
snuggle your breast
when the light
hurts me

your night
a warm blanket
enfolds me
in you

to sleep
in your soft arms
make the day
a mouse.

Anniversary '89

Hell of a year
Hell
of
a
year
sine wave
large amplitude
high frequency
riding the beam
leaves hands shaking
heart in triple time
almost went off the scale
a couple of times
up, two shows
down, death in NY
up, reading in NYC
down, no job
up, two articles, two reviews
down, mother-in-law hospitalized
up, down
up, down
quarks bound together
tied by God's law
what a pair
up and down
strange and charm
truth and beauty
me and you, kid
we survived
I think
Hell of a year

Hell
of
a
year

the annual ode
to us
another year
under our belts
hell of a year
death and productions
layoffs and etc.
muddling through
paying the toll
sticking together
somehow
holding on
holding on
to each other
when there's not much else
to hold on to
oh yes
it could be worse
it could be
without you.

1989

Thunder rides in
a season of storms
we curl together
against the night
year of lightning
flashes and strikes
you cover me
against the light
love is a holding
a struggling on
a rock in the wind
amidst the fight
time blows onward
sunshine and rain
bind us together
left and right.

What I'm Writing

I don't like what I'm writing these days
too much ice this winter
but dry, no gleaming snow with soft edges
just cold, hard, and silent
like writing with a knife.

In Deep Throat

In Deep Throat
    everybody gets laid
        nobody gets pregnant
        nobody has VD or AIDS
        nobody gets jealous

     nobody gets hurt
  everybody lives happily ever after

In Hansel and Gretel
   parents desert children
     children are caged
     children destroy houses
     children cause divorce
     children kill old women
  everybody lives happily ever after

Now you tell me
Which is the fairy tale.

Turning Away

Turning away
like a woman in bed
who wants to sleep
leaving me
to slowly chill
body heat ebbing away
one day you will cover me again
with earth and grass
and I, in the darkness
will remember
your turning away.

On the Fortieth

On the fortieth such occasion
I will not be there
A slice is packed in plastic
to eat between work and work
The woman will complain
The kid will cry
But I will not be there
until too late
for such occasions

So count your blessings
one by one
poor health, cold house
two jobs, big mortgage
big wife, small daughter
and forty hard years
of pain and struggle
to get somewhere
but I will not be there

And look to life
to time to come
middle-class poverty
the family burdens
hopes dying on vines
no ease until the day
I will not be there.

Winter

Winter's bad breath
icicles dripping
from my nose

artificial colors
of frozen life.

God's Millstone

God's millstone grinds on
ignorant of the corn
that yesterday
reached for the sun

time's water turns the wheel
and flows on
never knowing the stone
white as bone

heaven's rain, far away
falls on the mountain
unaware that down the stream
it will power the wheel

and in earth's field
the broken stalk
dries and dies
bereft of golden grain.

When the Knife

When the knife enters
      It burns
only the twist
      is pain
the bleeding
      delicious sleep
the rest
      forgotten dreams.

Life Prisoner

Will the life prisoner
claw the tunnel
when his fingers are worn off
will he chew the bars
when his teeth are gone
will he scribble messages on walls
when the blood has dried?
This jail has many endings
hard walls and steel doors
gibbets and insulated chairs
But the cruelest end
known to men
is to live on
behind the casket door.

Behind the Eyes

Behind the eyes
the fire burns low
clouds cover the sky
rain is heard
cold wind
night is falling
on the dim day
not much occurred
spark, flame, breeze
embers, ashes
behind the eyes.

In Brazil

In Brazil
there are no Christmas trees
only naked women
holding palm frons
over their breasts
with little lights
as they sway
to the rhythm
of the talking drums
beating out "O Come Ye . . ."
while the little boys
open the present
between the limbs
and eat the sweet
Christmas candy.

Between Waking and Sleeping

Between waking and sleeping
reason sublimates like dry ice
liquid thoughts
exist only in imagination
like the women in our dreams
who never were
between mother and wife
only rumors between realities
liquid carbon dioxide
possible
but never seen
in nature
waking dreams
in pressure chambers
of what seems.

Parts

Wednesday the 24th, 5:15, teeth
Monday the 5th, 3:30, eyes
part by part
a tune-up here
an oil change there
our vehicles are serviced
parts is parts
that never knew.

Metal Womb

In shiny metal womb
we travel
safe, baring miscarriage
from the world outside
heartbeats from the radio
floating on vulcanized fluid
fed by Exxon umbilical
knowing only dimly
the sounds of Mother Earth.

Life

Life
a sexually transmitted disease
ultimately fatal
with no known cure
or treatment
characterized
by gradual destruction of the body
long-term, low-grade pain
with occasional episodes

of spontaneous remission
usually not long-lasting
there are some antidotal cases of survival
but none are scientifically documented
it is highly infectious during intercourse
but otherwise difficult to transmit
the only known preventative is education
but even that is not highly effective
treatment is symptomatic
just make the poor bastards
as comfortable as you can
until it's over.

Murder Before Morning

Murder before morning
spring forward
fall back
dead
as a doornail
in the sunrise
before the white dew
causes you to slip
and admit
your crime
of passion fruit
and guava
that lovers eat
seductively
in bed
late at night
before the morning
dies at dawn.

Let Me State

Let me state
for the record
or tape
or CD
earning 6½ percent
of the base
on balls
will kill a pitcher
of lemonade
or first aid
and assistance
is necessary
and sufficient
to prove the theorem
states of mind
like Nebraska
corn huskers
and huskies
race through the snow
white and the seven
deadly sins
will send you to hell
on wheels
rolling down the highway
and by way
of Route 66
to the sea.

Snow White

Snow White and the Seven Deadly Sins
shacked up in the woods
until the Wicked Witch of the West
sold a bite of paradise

that sent her to dreamland
until Prince Charming ate her Adam's apple
(and other parts)
which is enough to wake even Sleeping Beauty
who let down her hair
and decided to swing a little
just as Red Riding Hood showed up
with the wine and a horny wolf
but the party really started at midnight
when Cinderella ran in
just as her gown turned to dust
and fell right off
leaving her wearing nothing but one spike heel
until another Prince ran in
with the other shoe and a royal hard-on

About nine the next morning
the pile of bodies began to untangle
just as Mother Goose came in
and set the orgy in motion again
once, twice, even three times
upon a time.

Modern Life

Lack of sleep makes you crazy
Lack of exercise kills you
Lack of stimulation makes you stupid
Lack of life makes you normal.

Titles

Acting Branch Chief, Department of Enlightenment: For Grants Helping Individuals Justify Keeping Low-Level Minions Nameless; Outside People Quizzical; Regional Stooges Tame; And Underrated Versatile Workers Xenophobic, Yielding, and Zapped.

Occupational Hazzard

I
was not designed
to sit
all day
at a desk
illuminated by CRT
and florescence
ignorant
of sun or rain

in my youth
I walked
everywhere
through snow in Arizona
in sandals
rain in Kentucky
in Nikes
I swam
in oceans
in Carolina
in pools
in Mississippi

now I sit
at a desk
in Georgia
atrophy
an occupational hazard
and wait
to die young.

In Kentucky

In Kentucky
winter strips the land
revealing its barren skin
pox-marked, bruised
until the snow
like a vice cop
covers the naked sin.

Sunrise at Sixty

Sunrise at sixty miles per hour
arching over stone overpasses
arcing over interstates
leaves red, yellow, gone
passed in glimpses
scenery seen at sixty
images imagined
lit in flashes
by the road of dreams.

Untitled

Time has passed its zenith
I have dug my own grave
And now await the night.

Seasons

Winter lays us bare
nude limbs in a cold sky
little left to hide

In this our fourth winter
we two are now three
joined and divided
multiplied and reduced

Each tree stands alone now
dancing in the strip joint
under the lights
and hard music

The bed is cold
we sleep in shifts
trying not to count
what we gave each other

Around the spring
at the heart of the stream
ice forms in cracks
and breaks the old stones

Seasons come and go quickly
mountains die more slowly
piece by exhausted piece

We stand between
giving up leaves one by one
standing like old trees
shading a sapling
from winter chills.

Cat's Eyes

Cat's eyes go out quietly
babies cry unknowingly
and my bed is cold

In Ethiopia
a child starves to death

I do not care

My cares are all committed
booked up till 1993
at least

I am never alone
work to class to cribside
again and again

My life is parceled out to others
over-sold, 110 percent of shares committed

The Black Death of the '90s comes
plague, pestilence, pollution

I do not care

One cat
One baby
One wife
That is all.

Months

It has been months
my mind is flabby
the writer's callus is soft
no way to live
perpetual dozing.

At Night

At night
I wake
straining
to hear
amplified
breathing
from the
next room
trying
to distinguish
my wife's snores
from the electric
baby breaths
whose silence
awakens me
in terror.

My Hands

My hands hurt
or go numb
from strain
the joints
already corrupted

by arthritis
cannot lift
and type
and hold my fear
all day
without losing
feeling.

Bone

Bone, my bone
you hurt
ache
deep in the joint
protective cartilage
worn away
calcium cut into groves
whimpering
of twisted, clumsy
days to come.

Still's

It is not your fault, Elizabeth
none of this was your idea
nobody asked your opinion
you didn't decide anything
it's not your fault
it's God who is cruel, or Fate, or genes
but not you
you did the best you could
and were very good
as babies go
so it's not your fault.

Now

I'm always tired now
Nine months of fatherhood
Have worn me to the bone
I don't sleep
I don't move
I sit at desks
      in cars
      in classrooms
Then go home
And hold a baby
      in a chair
      on a bed
      on the floor
I become soft
      tired
      weak
As she grows
      I fade
And no one cries
      but me.

Elizabeth's Eyes

The eyes are mine
the nose, cheeks, etc.
are from her mother
but the eyes are mine
and she haunts me
staring back at me
with my eyes
how much of me
can she see
with my eyes?

Failure

I don't want to think anymore
the thoughts are black and bloody
cancers and bleeding bank accounts
arthritis and aching years
failure footnoted in forgotten tomes.

Father's Day

On Father's Day
I installed a showerhead
spent the afternoon
taking the wife and daughter shopping
changed diapers, took out trash
cleaned the cat box
watered the plants
and received
a blue ribbon
for being
a good Dad.

Devoid of Windows

Devoid of windows
in his eyes
he sees darkness
in all directions
sunrise and noon
pass unmarked
until at evening
the door closes
unseen, unknown.

The Act of Writing

The act of writing
should spark ideas
Noel Coward
copied his name
over and over
until he thought
of something better
but Noel Coward
is an interesting name
I have no ideas
    no feelings
no dreams
    left
a shadow
anesthetized upon a table
not even watching
the women come and go
though I am told
even during heart surgery
the patient can hear
and remember
passing comments
about the scrub-nurses' second cousin
who is getting divorced
from some poor soul
who is devoid
of ideas, feelings
or dreams
and spends his life
copying his name
over and over
on important papers.

According to Regulations

According to the regulations
life should be typed
double spaced
in 10 pt. Courier
on 20 lb. paper
but somehow
Helvetica 30 pt. bold
keeps breaking out
on my printer.

The Words

The old poetic tricks don't work today
Sonnets just do not fit the times
The bards of old who sang a lay
Can't rock and roll or rap their lines
So Poe and Pope are 'round the bend
Compared to Guns N' Roses, Grateful Dead
Don't count iambs, don't even pretend
To care how strong stress is said
Count quarter time and beats to the bar
Top forty airplay, concert gross
To find the latest shooting star
Who thinks image, not words, is boss

And bless Paul Simon, Diamond, Byrds
Dylan, Lennon, and Cohen
For they remember words.

Painfully Obvious

It is painfully obvious
that my thoughts
are obviously plain
insights measured in centimeters
retinitis pigmentosa of the brain
a world shrunk to two small rooms
      both empty
except for things
and memories of dreams
that faded in the sunrise
no wisdom here
no revelation of the psyche
an empty man
scribbling on
like the mindless monkey
typing unmarked keys
hoping for Hamlet.

Interview

Park under the fifth floor
have your ticket stamped
check your fly
and above all
do not say anything smart.

Why Can't I

Why can't I write something?
For the first time in a year
I have time on my hands
And nothing comes, no ideas, no words
Nothing
Is it all gone?
Burned out somewhere
      in the fatigue
        and lack of exercise
Worn away by too many concerns
      by two jobs
          a baby
          a dying father
Where did it go?
Why did it leave?
What do I have to do to get it back?

Ellis Island

I went to Ellis Island
      in my dreams
So near and yet so far
El Diablo
The Illusion on the hill
That creeps away
      like fog
I saw the mists
The streets of gold
And boarded the ship
      for home.

Open Wide

Open wide
cut, yank
another piece of wisdom gone
surviving on ice cream
a foretaste
of toothless age
wisdom comes late
leaves early
our bite
all too brief.

The Turned Phrase

The turned phrase
turns on me
reflecting back
a darker eye

These days
just walking
takes effort
I used to flow
effortlessly
from hill
to hill
scene
to scene
now I watch
children run
as aimless
as my gaze

The T-shirt

on the actor
said
"My youth,
which way
did it go?"
It went
that-a-way
where time,
unlike a phrase,
never turns.

Date

Day: 212
Year: 91
Century: 20th
Age: A.D.
Epoch: of Futility
      (only in Latin).

Quiet

Quiet
is not heard
anymore
I live
in noise
voices
on phones
fingers
tapping keys
the static
of work
that interferes
with thought.

An Art

There is an art
to living tired
to waking up
while still asleep
to sleeping awake
to dying slowly
long day
by short night.

Dribs

Dribs, drabs, dribbles
She never heard of tribbles
Mish, mash, miece
Or even Edwin Meece

A slate as blank
As genes allow
Doesn't know souse from sow
And so I let her sleep.

My Father

Kidneys, lungs, liver
an English pie of organs
afflicted with too much life
Renal Cell Carcinoma
engaged in an orgy
divide and conquer
the frail body
that once, one cold night
over forty years ago
gave me life
Father, Dad, enemy
I love, not like
I never wanted
to be like you
never thought
you wise
and left
as soon as
you gave me money
even now
as life tightens
in your chest
I only dread
having to see you
I only hope
somewhere
you found something
sometime
you did not judge
and laughed
like I never saw.

Always Away

Elizabeth
you are doing very well
being cute for Mommy
growing too fast for her
claiming yourself
with little grasping hands
eating the world
edible or not
today you crawl
tomorrow you run
always away
always away.

Tapping

Tapping fingers
busy idle hands
indecisive rhythm
beating time.

Images

Videotapes, snapshots, photographic portraits
slicing life into images
bits of was
we were that
back then
reflected light and memory
if ever a then.

Food

Elizabeth is eating hash browns at daycare
I eat an apple at my desk
Kathy eats out
Food consumes us all.

Silence

In the silence
there is silence
so let me go now
me and I
to where
the patient sky
is ice
that will suffice
for quiet desperation
amidst the sounds
of silence.

The Head

The bones
of the cranium
are ten miles thick
and made of lead
the eyes
are tunnels
with no light
at the end
the ears
curve and spread
into infinite smallness
before closing
the mouth
is a sinkhole
filling with water
but no bottom
the head
is swollen
too heavy to lift
above the horizon.

What I Am

It creeps in at night
like twilight
listening to two females snore
some existential anguish
hits my gut
and twists
like an ulcer
festering inside
slowly burning my flesh
I am not what I become

and the paradox
like Maxwell's Demon
rips my breath away
I almost yell
I want to stamp both feet at once
kick my fate in the balls
change what might have been
I cannot sleep
no dreams for me
not one
the bars of obligation
the locks of practicality
the chairs of fear
the handcuffs of failure
I am what I am
and it is not enough.

My Daughter's First Vomiting

Her look said
what the hell is this
as vomit poured out
her nose and mouth
this is no milk spit-up
what is happening to me
are my insides coming out
does this happen often
is this growing up
why is this happening
what do I do now?

I changed the bed
Mommy changed the clothes
Life is full of little changes.

Fatherhood

My dreams
are full of dead babies
that silently ceased to breathe
and young girls
with innocent breasts
who love/hate boys
A year of terror
and fatherhood.

Of Laughter

Sounds of laughter in the hall
friendly conversation overheard
scrapes a childhood sore
that never healed
crowded hallways were
      and are
empty to me
bumper cars that dodge
      and run
as I spin counter
to the flow
suddenly the current stops
for now the ride is over
but my guts are still torn
hollowed out by sounds
that always come
through solid walls.

Afraid

I am afraid to touch her anymore
the cost is too high
and there is so little left
she has taken almost all
the innocent, loving thief
who hugs you to pick your pocket

Her breasts once mine
are full of milk
and for another

Her body, once full
is now fat
and tired

I paid my career
      my theatre
      my vacations
      my music
every moment, every dollar
I ever had
I cook, I clean, I wash, I shop

I got two women who cry at times
      smile at times, claim to love me

Then ask for more
than I will ever have
and don't even know it.

No Icepick Image

It seems like
all I do
is yawn
even on paper
no icepick image
or soap opera life
just borderline exhaustion
amid the same old same old
wearing down
like sandstone
in a stream
quietly becoming
none
with the universe.

Memories

It's strange the memories
one line of soda fountain dialogue
from nineteen sixty-nine
or an image of basement stairs
vintage nineteen seventy-six
hints of a life barely lived
fated to vanish with the man

They found a two-thousand-year-old man
frozen in a glacier
that melted this hot summer
what did he remember
of a life barely lived
now forgotten for the ages

at least of him

they will ask
and he a stupid hunter
who died in a fall.

Proper Nouns

Decisions are made quietly
in empty rooms
by proper nouns
Verbs may spring the doors
daunt the trees
careen outside
be criticized
by adverb clowns
but decisions
are made quietly
in empty rooms
by proper nouns.

Time

Time passes
like a snail
crawling
inching
down the Concorde's aisle
at Mach 1 point 2
plus
three inches an hour
barely moving
from seat to seat
New York to Paris
origin to terminus
such agonizing slowness
on the fastest
of journeys.

September Favor

Do me a September favor
Falling loose from your limbs
Let it go, be bare before me
Show turn of trunk
Grain of light brown bark
Sway slowly in the wind
Shiver in the cool breeze
Whisper to me of sunny days
Of cool nights, of summer gone
Of winter yet to come. Show me
What nature intended for you today
Let me see the seasons we share
Let me see the reasons we dare
Face the coming cold.

Lost Persona

Shredded paper
wadded up
tossed away
into the gutter
gets rained on
coagulates
into a lump
of dyed cellulose
decomposes
rots
and dies

the words
it held
unknown
forever lost.

The Pool

The bronze bikini girls bake
by the pool beside my apartment
asses or tits thrust upward
barely covered from burning sun.
No one swims.
It is an exercise of burning youth
to ashes of soft bodies and hard skins.
They bask in burnished glory,
posing as I stroll by,
musing of even barer bodies
in the faceless sex of dreams,
the eternal fantasy of undeserved love.
The nightmare stares us in the face.
They are burning for beauty
and the blessings beauty brings.
I am burning for dreams
that bless the dreamer
before only ashes
are left to sing.

Evening Stroll

Light falls like rose petals
upon the town beneath
no dog whimpers to mar
the evening breeze
the fat T-shirt
sits in the drive
to cool and repeat
the evening rite
kids babble in the street
ageless ritual jokes
we pass in stride
consuming what we eat
staring at glass eyes
that see in and out
who lives who dies
what sex is sung
revolts run to earth
as evening comes
the simple street
of toys and guns
of proud cars and raw grass
much unsung blood
the corner turned
repeat repeat the street.

Eyes

There are no horrors left
the Holocaust, Cambodia
Kennedy, King, wounded Wallace, Pope
boned Ethiopia, wired Argentina
even Hiroshima, Nagasaki ashes
Palestine sells fear for dimes

Mother Russia gulags her sons
and petty men bleed petty crimes
scared inhabits modern eyes
but horror is defunct
roaches will inherit, maybe ants
buttons can be pushed
eyes sliced open clean
the womb can feel a jagged edge
babies fed to bees
horror comes only from surprise
that such a thing can be
what eyes my eyes have seen
know such a thing could be.

Sunny Lines

I sit inside on summer days
and try to think of sunny lines
that rhyme or rhythm set
or freer verse by reason so declined
in warmer climes however
often thunderclouds darken view
metaphors thunder rather than shine
similes strike, not glow
so versed in storm am I
of cloud tears running rivulets down
of rushing, chilling, windy themes
that even on burning, blueish days
beyond the horizon
my eyes see gathering, grayish clouds.

Four Years

And now we are three
a "family"
but this anniversary
I will not calculate
gains and losses
(the calculus of constant change
I have long forgot)
we are three now
two united in a new way
made one flesh
numbers enough

Roses, lilies, and babies bloom
Love, hard and strange
puts roots through rock
exhausting, painful growth
toward an unexpected sky

we are here
we are together
we are three.

So Caesar Said

The Druids, so Caesar said
sacrificed their mortal foes
in wooden cages of flesh and flame
to stately oaks and balls of mistletoe
he thought that not quite right
but he was sliced to bits
on sacred ground in Senate hall
by friends and fellow countrymen
who prayed on Power's lowly alter
so Caesar had no right to talk.

The Gun-hand

The gun-hand shakes
The head jerks away
from inside pitches
The foot lifts off the throttle
way before the turn
In short, the belief is gone.
Darkness crawls over the still figure
like ants
Something is being eaten away
Bridges, stone and iron,
fall suddenly, unsuspected,
run over one time too many
The fallen gladiator, in pain,
breathes dust and waits,
knowing he was not good enough
Empty eyes that looked inside
living skulls with empty eyes
that saw too little
Most men fail
Most dreams die
Timing is everything.

Christmas Vision

It was Christmas
the afternoon lull
past presents
and filling meal
I sat to watch some ballgame
my mother lay on the couch
to nap
during some aftershave ad
I glanced at her
Death had touched her face
she lay, arms crossed
as if . . .
This is how
she will look
I thought
when . . .
face sagged smooth
still
gone
resting in the arms of . . .
a nap
for her
I will be the one
who stares into the face

the rise and fall
of her stomach
reassured me
but the image
remains
Age and Time

new fears
now named.

Convention

The Democrats to the Atlanta went
Republicans to New Orleans did fly
To eat and drink and scream
and shout till spent
Then see who else they could
with power buy
A game! A race! A Party parties hardy
Three thousand chant, three thousand dance
and wave
their signs while grinning happy like a smarty
"We're on TV, we're wild and free, we save
the country quarterly, we have no sin
we're gonna win, we love our man,
he's just
the savior called for in this looney bin."
And so it goes, the Emperor's clothes are wove
Till all stand nude before new Hitler's stove.

Birth

Black life crawls out
draining dreams
Death of birth
Birth of death
Passing a torch
of pain
Is any man as guilty
as when he condemns
his own son to life
and himself
to fading
for another
Death drives us to birth
Better we quietly die
than infect another soul
There is no purgatory
only life
That is hell enough
Why inflict it
on another
and call it love?

Done and Done

Done and done, you go, I stay
or the other way, or not. One or
two or three, together alone
here, there, no matter. At night
you only warm one side of me
Self-centered? Yes, I cannot stand
where my feet are not. My shoes
are not empty, you cannot walk in them
I have seen what I have seen

heard the nightingale sing; you,
a budgie or canary hear, caged parakeet
You dream of new life, I live an
old dream. Our lives osculate
intersect, penetrate, but in geometric hell
never converge. There is an axiom
of time, it moves forward, we see back
and what is done is done. Done
and done.

New Life

An awesome thing, new life, from penis to
the cervix, up the tube to ovary
and back again in pain to giggles, goos
to toddler, tot, and off to school
then dates, hot nights, and wedding vows
and one more song of sex as sperm to ovum go
again, same song, second verse, granddad, grandson
grand time was had by all, so small a note
discordant sounds amid the chorus loud
A god was wise it seems to make the penis blind
and hide the cervix in a darkened room
too much pain shines beyond
so those who live by eyes would never shout
Encore! Encore! but quietly and one
by one at intermission fade.

Choices

You don't get many choices in this life
and most are devil or the deep blue sea,
of rocks or places hard, of frying pans or fires,
of wife's too-frozen silence or a baby's squalls
no music here, no jigs or squares to call
us from toil. Bitter tastes, garlic tears,
attic odors, the poor man's faded sight.
Choose, choose! blind canyons, darker caves,
tigers behind every door, wearing veils and curls
the eaten man may cry a warning
but the dark pit is irresistible
We all go in to win the princess
Never remembering the year-king
Never remembering that the fertility god
has to die.

Geometry

Euclid believed in flat

Pythagoras believed in
               right
                 angles

Descartes was
for   grids

                  time
  Einstein
                      relative
        space
            as
   saw

Not the Same

There's fucking
having sex
making love
and making babies

fucking is fun, delightful, enjoyed by old and young
having sex satisfies drives, calmly sates instinct
making love caresses, cares, kisses, comforts, binds
making babies ties, incurs, obligates, obliges, creates
something between you
that grips both sets of hands
and pushes out.

Unprotected Sex

Unprotected sex
a new thing
to post-pill babies
now YUPs, ringed, paired
with ticking bio clocks
Deliberate choices
not burst balloons
not slipped (latex) disks
not reasonless passion
Sliding into the dark unknown
coin into slot
take your chances
what will emerge
Gamblers with life
placing bio bets
worth hundreds of thousands
winner lose all
For a smile, giggle, tiny love
something to come home to
to be the mommy/daddy
to have a child
To pass along the pain.

About Their Hair

Listening to women talk about their hair
the amazing triviality
of frizzes and curls
sets and perms
tints and tones
tie-dyes and tinsel
for all I know
like a poodle on parade
it's not for men
men want hair
you can run in
or through
so why the endless verbiage
of cornrow versus beehive
ending splits or ironing curls
off the shoulder, in the ear
pageboy, punk, perfumed, preened
pray tell me, ladies
simple, clear
without pretense, evasion
is all the primping, posing, permanenting
for vanity and pride
or getting topics
for discoursing?

In an Office

There's not much to write about in an office
the ruler on the wall
        is straight
        metal
        cool
the computer/monitor
        is square
        plastic
        warm
the desk
        flat
pens
        round
phone
        silent
tape
        sticky
clips
        bent
paper
        blank
light
        on
employee
        bored

and that's about it, folks.

The Winter

Now begins the winter
of our discontent
as the dry fall
fears what may befall
before the tardy spring
Let us our lessons learn
scholars of the frost
When gods can cause icefall
men's lives are not their own
Frigid, unfurrowed ground
births brambles in the spring
Silent cold kills flowers
in the heart and in the ground
In the long, quiet nights
hearth fires both blaze and to ashes turn
Finally, in the blossom bud green time
some emerge to warm
and share hot life
in seasons yet to come
and some, victims of the embracing snow
are never found.

High Rise

The evil of office buildings
glassed from roof to ground
is that the peons of pencil pushers
inhabit inner lands
far from horizon-fading vistas
envious of the favored few
who on circumference sit
seeing far, fantastic, futuristic
while lesser lights
have not even old frame
or pane of glass
no hint of sun's pacing pass
no brightening or dimming of sight
no beam across the floor
no dancing dust specks taking flight
we get an artificial day
that makes surprise of night

so like the roses grown inside
we're weak, susceptible to blight
thinking gods are little men
who turn off and on the light.

August

It is August
the leaves in my driveway yellow are
dry and brittle
doomed to sight
a dry year
when leaves die
before the season turns
pleasant, stable

the weather was
sunny and warm
fine future forecast
day after day
a regular paycheck
so dependable, secure
count on established, steady days
warm sun, cloudless blue
umbrella dusty, forgotten
in easy, sunny Summer
until it August is
and the leaves
in my driveway
yellow are.

Ease Him Gently

Ease him gently into life
my son or daughter
who to be
Life begins in pain and tears
and ends the same
a light beginning let it be
and end the same
and in between
though much the same
may they remember this
a bright beginning we begot
as best we could, a kiss
a prayer, a hope for this
they would be glad we beginning gave
before into the mist we fade.

The Day

The sunrise hid in mists today
creeping up when none could see
we only knew it by the whiter fog
that slowly turned from black to gray
but staring east with painless eyes
no orb or arc could see
by noon, no doubt, the mist will flame
exposing bluer, plainer skies
and yellowed torch supreme
no open eye can see
until this eve as dark befall
one last glimpse the day redeem.

The Addicted

In my unsmoking office
the addicted
hide in the aptly named firestairs
like schoolgirls
sneaking to the john
to consume a bite of forbidden, tasty death
grown men and women
with MAs and Maseratis
huddle together
on stone steps
littered with their own ashes
medicated by ether
bound by brownish leaves
self-respect their victim
they grovel on the stone.

Post-its

Post-its are pieces of paper
packed in pads
of yellow or blue
and sticky behind
so notes
of extraordinary import
or crucial report
will stick
outside your mind.

Little Dreams

You have such little dreams
Me every night
A baby
live long and easy
one room every night
is this all for you?

the mail mistress
       knows all, tells all
what I dream for you
       beauty undeniable
       wild nights
       my arm in flashing lights
       biographer's notations
       grief/joy renowned
       pain/pleasure famed
       the long run to dark

Yours may be the wiser dream
if less to glory suited
but don't you know no racer runs
who never chase has started.

Untitled

All Betty can do even from good home
is just keep looking, moving now
over plain, quiet room, seeing through
utter vision with X-ray, your zipper.

The Wilder Dance

You fear beauty
I know that
and hide it
neath candy flab
and chocolate
youth is gone now too
so much is past
I cry a tear for you
who slept through dreams
and sat out
the wilder dance.

Among the Sadder

Among the sadder things in life
are vacant mailboxes
and unringing phones
the touch of technology
that leaves us empty hands.

My Eyes Water

My eyes water
whenever I close them
(except in sleep

but even in prayer)
as if crying
over visions missed.

Paper Clips and Rubber Bands

Paper clips and rubber bands
hold the world together
glue to patch the torn and ripped
staples, tape, notebook, binders
anything to save it all
from tearing, obscene fingers
we are our own destroyers
who scatter, lose
what we create
but for the few
who clip and file
our story safe from danger.

Untitled

Erect in chair
arms crossed
head up
eyes closed
sleeping
sitting upright
tiptoeing the line
tween here and there
alert body
darkened mind
not even twenty winks
not even ten
just two or three
a moment's night
and then . . .

Trick

This is words
Hot and cold
Ice or fire
So some secret
Is hidden inside
So before, behind
Not known, but seen
Or heard by some
Tricks play on minds
Arcs of meaning turn
Piece by piece the puzzle
Opens to those who learn
Enough to know
Much is not what seems.

Anagrams

Anagrams
New or old
Are exercises
Growing mental muscles
Reaching, stretching
Are warmups for
More trying
Strenuous tasks.

Not Quite

Computer keyboard clicks
      crunch not like leaves
Forced air circulation
      sings not like breeze
Elevator signal rings
      are not larksong
Telephones buzz
      but not like bees
Even glowing lights
      Are not the sun
So denizens of office deeps
      are not quite men.

Soho

Soho like a signal lays
not far from mighty Thames
and Donavan, whose deed is done
is now a singing hymns
farther down the path
Mick's turned gray
Herman's trying opera
Dave Clarks only one again
here and there a gravestone head
a Jim, a John
a time, a day, passed away
Strawberry Fields forever.

My Wife's Diets

My wife's diets
make me hungry
sympathetic pains
induced by lettuce
and Brussel sprouts
(which I hate)
you can't feast
before a faster
nor dine well
on celery fare
naturally slim I
(thank you God)
long since despairing
of saving snacks
from her searching eye
just hope and pray
she'll become thin
before my bones
say hello to my skin.

Bologna

Bologna and orange
my luncheon fare
crunched in cubical office
feasting on despair.

Writing

Grind it out
Put letter after letter
Verse after verse

Cut, carve, scrape
Pull that poem
Kicking and screaming
To birth.

Edge

I have written
my pen point
down to a nub
felt tip rubbed
to bare metal
giving my lines
a harder edge.

In the Dark

In the dark
of the knight's night
his nose knows
a sox's sock
as his page's page
to arm his arms
to mount his mount
and hie high
into the hills.

FYI

FYI
HRH
Has
ESP
For IUDs.

Amanda

A is for apple they'll tell you someday
Maybe for apricot, or alpha or
Above average, or anything at all
None of that is true
Don't believe a word of it
A is for you.

(For Amanda Wengen upon the occasion of her christening.)

Make Your Bed Early

Make your bed early
In love may you sleep
Close by the side
Here may you keep
All loves are easy
Each one by one
Leaving out none.

Seasons

Caress me a spring flower
that wakes, sparkles to bees
and in soaks the sun
before its day departs
Kiss me suddenly summer
warm and wet and wild
smiling some old psalm
of seasons sliding into years
On me gently fall
turning to me in the sunset
as tree to earth returns

in the passing of the tears
Embrace me warmly as winter fire
wearing flames in hearthstone hues
finding fine fierce surgings
through darkest eves in times to end.

Poetry

Nothing rhymes with orange
Except perhaps door hinge
Even worse is rhyming month
Without a lisping once
So never sing of girls named Ann
And forever let there be a ban
On sonnets that dare begin
"As I was eating my Ann's juicy orange
It came to me I love Ann and this month."

So go from there if you can
But don't blame me if you don't understand
That poetic suicide is a venal sin.

Twenty Years

Twenty years
after my cat has died
I will still be finding
cat hairs
on my
clothes.

Night

Drifting to sleep
like spoons
arm around you
breast in hand
I understand
suttee.

See This

See this?
Want to see it again?
Watch closely now.
There!
Did you see it?
Did you see the world end?
Or do you want me
To do it again?

I Like to See You Naked

I like to see you naked
Sitting at the breakfast table
Eating Corn Chex
It seems so healthy.

Damn Cute

You better be damn cute
That's all I can say
You better be damn cute
To take all my money
      my time

>   my sleep
>   my life
> The minute the doc said yes
> I had to start hustling
> > moonlighting
> > pinching
> And you no bigger than a pinhead
> Everybody's happy but me
> I'm just tired
> Maybe sick
> Certainly scared
> So you better be damn cute.

Dreamkiller

The dreamkiller
will arrive
on the big four-oh
finally committing me
half gone
to my father's fate
to a silent Greek tragedy
to be Shakespeare's little brother
never born
never made
he died in childbirth
in blood and pain
and never cried
poor little thing.

Conversion

You can't count on conversion
Word to Perfect
or vice versa
sometimes a bit is lost
and the message isn't saved
exactly
conversion to conversion
convert to convert
the fidelity is lost
until the screen is filled
with a distorted word
that changes everything.

For the Record

Just for the record
You weren't my idea
Your mother threatened me
     with leaving
So I took a chance
And drew you
I never was a gambling man
I always knew I'd lose
I hope you surprise me
But, for the record
You're a gamble
I didn't want.

Not Well

I am not well
body or soul
the future tires me
I have not the stomach
my bones ache
tomorrow's fatigue
kills me now
and in that sleep
no dreams may come

I did not mean to end thus
a slave at forty
bound and gagged
chaired and chained
little left of me
but duty
obligation
and silent tears

Caught
between solitude
and a stone
hemmed in
a devil
and an empty sea
no words here
no sound
just time
taking
taken
tomorrow
gone.

Within Three Walls

Within three walls
five feet high
terminal
telephone
tablets
time
fluorescent light
forced air
folders
fate
and the prisoner
in carrel #2
waits
for Apollo's lance
which never comes.

In the February

In the February
white and brittle
new life blows
reds and purples
In the October
Life will turn
Again to winter
Browns and grays
A cycle
so they say
the endless mystery
of life
What is never spoken
is the pain
of the broken limb

The aged, twisted tree
seeing the acorn
who has never known the lightning
      heard the thunder
      felt the hail
      bent the wind
      burned the sun
Sprout
thinking only May
never dreaming December.

This

You do not deserve this
No one deserves this
to see the fear
in eyes
that made you
apologies are worthless
explanations vain
you had no choice
but I did
what I lacked
was courage
I feared the silent streets
and so, you
who did not deserve this
not this
this
      life.

I Will Sing

Yes, I will sing
but
a sad song
a blues, perhaps
but without the rage
softly, without feeling
a hurt long gone
from another day
a little jazz echo
behind a lone guitar
six strings
plastic
imitation guts
hollow inside
to swell the sound
with sympathetic vibrations
can you hear it cry?
like the wind
from a train
long gone
just missed.

Don't Read This

Don't read this
word might get out
someone might hear
years from now
when the act was over
they might find out
what a thespian
I really was
and turn melodrama
into tragedy

Instead, hide this
set it aside
someday, two generations hence
the blood will be gone
and these lines
can be painlessly
forgotten
as the oddity
of a bitter old man
who never wanted
this.

Oedipus Eyes

We had
Vietnam for breakfast
The Killing Fields for lunch
The Sudan for dinner
For snacks
We ate Hinkley
And Speck
At midnight
A bite of Bundy
Before sleep
Cast iron stomachs
No Pepto in sight
If it bleeds
It leads
And poor poets
Stare at Oedipus eyes
That have seen too much
And will not blink.

The Reef

The reef
hides
under the waves
honing its razors
edging upward
year by year
until the hull
crosses its blade
impaling itself
on the deadly
skeletons.

Black Ice

Black ice cuts
the highway
bleeding a chassis
into the ditch

Soon the corpse
is towed away
to a graveyard
to decompose

Stacked like cordwood
among other bodies
with rust-red scabs
and broken frames

A few body parts
transplanted
the rest returned
to the birth fire.

What Gets Said

Did you ever wonder
what gets said
in the dressing room
of a strip club
Do the dancers
as they attire
for disrobing
count the house
Are men disparaged
in crude, vile terms
or evaluated
based on wallet size
Perhaps it's just
another kind of office
full of gossip, cookies
and pictures of kids
Is there shop talk of
a new way to shake it
or envy of the new kid
not yet on a diet
Do they ever
talk of sex
or is that taboo
among the nude?

By the Time

By the time
the euphemisms
are all in
the meaning is gone

A discordant couple
exchanging body fluids
is not
pissed-off lovers
peeing on each other
but it sure
sounds that way

And an intravenous drug user
with non-sterile paraphernalia
sounds more like a strung-out trucker
who thinks he's a stud
than a junkie shooting up
with a dirty needle

There's many an ass
who doesn't know
what his rectum is
and many a cocksucker
who never heard of fellatio
and many a bureaucrat
who isn't aware
he's a fool.

Looking Like

Looking like
instead of being
is no substitute
for a true illusion
which appears
to be
an illusion
and is.

The Morning Came

The morning came
all over her face
as the cock
became erect and crowed
the sunrise
the earth spread herself
opening to the thrusts
of sunshine
baring her breasts
to the warm caress
feeling the touch
of the sun
on naked ground.

Updated Rhymes

Twiddle dee
and twiddle dumb
twiddled their thumbs
till they couldn't strum
fiddle dee dee
one two three.

Rub a dub dub
three men in a tub
were arrested for
criminal sodomy
and contorting
without a license.

Jack Sprat could eat no fat
His wife could eat no lean
Until their psychiatrist prescribed
A massive dose of thiazine.

Little Miss Muffet
sat on a tuffet
eating her curds and whey
until a dietician
said the RDA's revision
outlawed both curds and whey.

Mary had a little lamb
It's fleece was white as snow
Then the health inspector said
You're in the city limits now
The lamb has got to go
So Mary got a small goldfish
And everywhere that Mary went
The fish stayed home alone.

More Haiku

The pebble splashes
      in the empty garden pond
Silence in the wind.

Mountains now are green
      birds on wing survey the scene
And sing up a spring.

I can call the moon
      but it will not come to me
The gods know better.

Why are pebbles round
      after eons in a stream?
Time has no edges.

Inside a black hole
      eternity stops forever
Never starts again.

Anniversary 6

Six years
parents two
gutting it out
no glory
hard love now
the rock endures
can you count to six?
I count on you
count on me
like counting on toes
callused, smelly, sore
but there
ready for the next step.

Too Young

I am too young
to be reading obituaries
in newspapers, professional journals
and alumni newsletters
we should be dying
in car crashes
to everyone's surprise
not of pneumonia
as expected
but the black of ink
confirms
what is under the lines
we are losing ourselves
too soon
too soon.

Stripper

The statuesque young woman
wearing a jacket
with the logo
of the local strip bar
sat at McDonald's
with her two daughters
eating a burger, fries
and an apple pie.

Biopsy

Mortality struck at four o'clock
by phone
a little brown freckle
renamed carcinoma
under the microscope
called to say
you too shall pass
do not count your years
until the candles are on the cake
that little girl
may grow up without you
retirement may never come
enjoy the rosebuds
while they bloom
come back Thursday at two
and we will cut you.

Scott

His name was Scott Heumann
>   (pronounced Hy-man)
He knew more about English literature
>   when he started college
than most English majors do
>   when they finish
but when he wanted help
>   editing a literary journal
he asked a physics major
>   (we were freshmen)
and I was his coeditor
>   for two and a half years
and friend for four

He was gay, I was not
>   but we sang opera together (yes, opera)
>   edited and printed each other's poetry
>   and ate supper together in the refectory
>   almost every night the first year or two
I learned criticism, theatre, and
>   humility from him
what he learned from me, god knows

Something in his MA work (at another school)
>   soured him on academia
After a stint as a journalist
>   he became a dramaturg
>   for an opera company
>   (he probably loved that)
And died not long before
>   the twentieth alumni reunion
AIDS? Car crash? I don't know

      the alumni paper just said
      "In Memorandum"
As if I could forget
      my friend.

Generations

Watching my mother and daughter
      clearing the dinner table
Time, defying Einstein
      summersaults
I see my mother young
      my daughter old
My mother is twenty-five again
      near the end of the war
Newly married, happy
      in Oklahoma
Not bent by ill children
      and a difficult man
My daughter is also twenty-five
      suddenly mature
Beautiful, but with sad eyes
      having seen too much
Wondering what loads
      will weigh her down
And I stand between
      seeing both visions
Eyes wet for what was
      and what will be.

Parenthood

Parenthood opposes poetry
clear lines leap not from hazy minds
that seek lost sleep in quiet times
that once filled brains with energy

"Diaper" and "potty" fit no refrain
though tiny hands and hugs inspire
though cute the curl or soft the smile
out of baby's reach, my pen is lain

So cuddle on my lap, my love
it's Mother Goose's time to shine
so ask not from my treasure trove
for Daddy's out of rhyme.

Cleveland

Is flatter than the lake
Its houses all in rows
Its trees have pulled up stakes
For lands of lesser snows.

Sleep

Elizabeth will not sleep alone
She wants her blankie
        dolly
        Mom
        and Dad
    green slippers on the colder nights
    two stuffed dinosaurs
    a monster or two

   Mickey and Minnie Mouse
     (in doll and puppet versions)
  At least three stories read just right
     (pillows, blankets, sheets, of course)
And then
   though barely three years old
She will not, though all about her snore
   or moan
deign to fall asleep
   afore ten.

Seeing My Daughter

Seeing my daughter silhouetted against the window
As she watched the leaves fall on the porch roof below
I, corny as it seems, thought about the falling days
My days turning gold or brown, hers only budding
But all falling away in the chilling wind.

Elizabeth

Laughter chasing bubbles
   in the wind

Joy catching a ball
   in outstretched hand

Peace sleeping quietly
   in my arms.

Coach, a Cat

There's no time for crying
not even for kitty cats
that a little girl kissed
and snuggled like a pillow
but lost to sleep
like a memory
of toddler times
fading through the years.

Direction

Turn left at Topeka
right at Abilene
then double back
through Santa Fe
follow the compass
not the road
measure the miles
in kilometers
and stop
when you reach ten thousand
then turn around
in your tracks
and see
where you've been.

Two Yesterdays

Take two yesterdays
half an hour
a dozen springs
two sunsets

one dawn
three moons or months
and season to taste
with time
mix well
bake at 98.6
for eighty-seven years
let cool
and serve.

Simple Simon

Time, time, time
see what's become of me
as I look around
there are no possibilities
there is no way to please
look around
life is brown
there's a batch
of pain
in a frown.

If the Sum

If the sum
from negative infinity
to positive infinity
is zero
does this mean
infinity is empty
or just equally
good and bad?

Merger

The Center for Urban Native Technology
has merged with
the Center for Offshore Communication Kinetics
to form the
Foundation for Urban Communication Kinetics
which is located in the
Agency for Social Societies
until the
Congressionally Unregulated Mandate
arrives.

Ad Infinitum

The Ad Infinitum
It's not just a car
It's an automobile
Like the breeze in the trees
Like the waves on the seas
It brings new definition
To the word expensive
The Ad Infinitum
It's not just a car
It's an automobile.

Hardly-A-Ford

Howdy, folks
Tom Hardly here, for Hardly-A-Ford
If you're a red-blooded American
you want an American car
not something built by a bunch of Japs or Huns
no matter how good it is

Well, up here at Hardly-A-Ford
we've got real American cars
      built by real American nigras
      up in Detroit
We're located up here in the mountains
      where our heads are low
      and everything's cheap
So come see us at Christmas
      when we're all lit up
And remember, if you're going to do it
      do it to the Hardly boys.

BC

PC crash? That's a BC headache
WC won't flush? That's a BC headache
Head hurts so bad you can't see?
    Take BC
In pain from listening to me?
    Take BC
BC headache powders
Tastes so bad
You forget your head.

Hey, Kids

Hey, kids
    Home from school?
    Want to play around a little
        but not get caught?
Get new Kiddie Condoms
    Specially made for growing boys and girls
Packaged to look just like bubble gum
    Kiddie Condoms
In the toy section of your drugstore
    Kiddie Condoms
Get yours now.

Ultrasound

The skull/face swims up
out of the ultrasound
boney eye sockets
fixed smile
freeze frame
print out
the first look
at my child-to-be
the nurse cuts
the snapshot sized
laser print
from the machine
and hands it to me
like a picture
for my wallet
at four months
more a frog
than human

I sit and stare
it looks back
with empty eyes.

To Elizabeth, before Her Birth

I have started watching
    the little girls
        before church
Wondering if you
    will sit quietly
        in frilly dress
Or scamper off
    to kick around
        with the boys
What will your smile be like?
Your hair, short or long?
Will you hug my leg
    as some girls
        do their fathers
Will your eyes sparkle
    blue or brown
        under bangs
Will you really love
    a bald old man
        with sad eyes?

My Father

My father
is dying
a little faster
than the rest of us

Sharp knives
and long
chemical poisons
only slow the black dancer

His whole life
he did everything
deliberately, perfectly
no matter how long it took

I suspect
he will deal
with dying
the same.

Dance

The black-masked dancer
digs the grave in darkness
shoveling the dank earth
into a mound
beside the grave
Deep in the hole
there is a silent treasure
dearer than gold
and twice as old
a prize all men die for
below the bottomless hole

beyond the beneath
is another dance
a dance done only
on the other side
of graves.

One Coming In

One coming in
one going out
one to remain
no fortunate one
one enters the veil
one exits the scene
one stands onstage
two masks in hand
no sure whether
to laugh or cry.

Blood is Red

If the blood is red
life is a problem
blood, sweat, or tears
we are born in blood
we sweat through life
we die in tears
and in between
the blood is red
the sweat is hot
the tears are mean.

The Pain

The pain
    is in the writing hand
the fatigue
    is in the back
the soreness
    in the arms
the ache
    in a deeper place.

Break Room

Take one free
For service call
Please allow money
If you empty
Served in cans
Will jam machine
For less.

Glaring

My mind and eyes
no longer sleep together
but each separately
closes on darkness
leaving the other
glaring at time to come.

Cold Eyes

Cold eyes
laugh

at little things
enjoying small adventures
closing
to events
that alter lives
birth, death
what are these
compared to puns
new sounds, new tastes
new sights
for cold eyes.

Elizabeth

Elizabeth, can you feel it
when I rub your mother's tummy?
Is that harder area
below her navel your head?
Is my hand there at all
or do you swim unaware
that someone, somewhere
wants to calm you
the only way he knows how.

Come

Come
run the wind
down yellow canyon
turn with the leaves
dance with the dawn
the day is coming
the wind will end
the leaves will fall
dawn will not light
the canyon wall.

Yesterday Will Not Come

Calling yesterday will not come
Knives scar tables and flesh
Time's edge is honed
        to a microsecond
Like a heavy bag
You take the punches
You have no choice
It's what you do
        absorb, absorb
Sand runs out slowly
        micropores, entropy
        empathy is lost
Take the bones
        there're all you have
        of yesterday's skeleton
The dawn also rises
        on the undead
Not requested, just there
Like everything else
You have to take it
Stare it in the eye
        and go blind
Like everybody else
        who has seen
        the sun.

Down by the Riverside

Hear the Salvation Army Band
walking on the wild side
lust for the bass drummer
with the big boobs
thumping out a rhythm

as old as sex
sing a song of succubi
sailors far from port
dream of demons and grow hard
it is not evil we seek
it is salvation, eternity
drumming like a heartbeat
cradled in lower lips
open to the maker of us all.

Service Call

Take one service call
fill with lead
from a pencil
that writes gray
once used by
the man who
seduced your great-grandmother
in Italy
on her honeymoon
before her father died
of grief
and call me
tell me your secrets
and bathroom habits
cough twice in the morning
and pay by check
I'll file the insurance
on your life
before anybody laughs
you'll never know
it won't hurt a bit
not even when
the pencil breaks
another hymen.

After

After my father's funeral
I'll screw my wife
if the baby is not there
This is not enough
it never is
there's nothing left
not even good memories
just ice that never melts
cold days in somewhere
heaven won't be quite right
not what he paid for
not up to his standards
too many colors
too few rules
not done his way
and I'll be left
with no choices
and few hopes.

Writer's Block

Noel Coward
wrote his name
over and over
until he thought
of something better
to write
but Noel Coward's
an interesting name.

Black Pavement

Black pavement
white mists
dead rain
rising
to meet
its maker.

Nick Weber

Nick Weber
who played piano
in 1973
is dead
In Memorandum
alumni review
no explanation
just a memory
of a stage
a piano
and a tune
in memorandum.

For This Life

The strands of gray
do not match
her swollen belly
I am bald
we are too old
    for this
        this life
        new
        small
        unborn
There is no time
    for this
    tardy birth
We should have
done this
twenty years ago
before we
    even met.

Untitled

Eight down
one to go
razors are painless
children not so.

First Fruits

Who calls the lazy flower to birth
It is too hot in August to even die
The sins of winter bear fruit in fall
We are all our parents' punishments
Bright red apples with slow poison
The fig leaf itches, and we eat
The first fruit of paradise was Cain
Infants are born to kill and die
Planting the first fruits of their labor
      Six feet under
Even Adam died alone, far from solitude.

Black Ink

It's strange how black ink
on black paper
dries to purple
as if there were enough darkness
to bleed dried blood.

Little Things

I have a little list
of little things to do
and one by one
each little thing
I make each one come true
and in a little while
I look back at my little list
and see how many little things
combine just bit by bit
to make a little life.

C-section

They say I can watch
when they cut her open
to pull out the child
bloody, screaming, and very surprised
at the short-cut
I'm sure it will be a wonderful sight
Placenta, uterus, intestines, and all
just the image to endear
father to child
at that wondrous moment
of surgical incision.

The Baby

The baby on the other side of the glass
its life still measured in minutes
opens its salved eyes
and stares at me
asking
where am I
what have you done to me
what did I do to deserve this?

Jim and Tammy

Jim and Tammy
had a show
that sold a cross
for a billion gross
so Praise the Lord
and pass the yacht
come ride the waterslide

just send in seventy-five
So Tammy got high
but wouldn't go down
on Jim so Jessie did
then tarts and Joes
what a life
take my wife
cue the condominium
Keep those checks coming in
There's blackmail to pay
poor in Palm Springs to help
pantyhose to sell
timeshare with Jesus, $5000 down
Curse those sinners
Get rich as a bitch
Live like there ain't no hell
Isn't religion wonderful?

To the Tune Of

Oral, Oral, are you praying
are you praying in the tower
in the tower? A sixty-foot-high Jesus
yes, a sixty-foot-high Jesus
wants you dead, wants you dead
better raise some money
better raise some money
'bout eight mil, 'bout eight mil
Oral, Oral, are you fasting
are you fasting between meals
between meals? Have them send the money
yes, have them send the money
save your soul, save your soul
better ask for mercy
better ask for mercy
you'll go to hell, go to hell.

Communication

And it's, like, well, OK, you know?
so I said, all right, like, see?
but she said, uh, no, like, well, you know?
OK, OK, I said, like, fine, sure.
You just, like, you know, don't get me,
and I'm, like, talking, you know,
so, OK, like, it's not my, you know, fault
if you can't, like, understand, you know?

Spoken

Words
Sounds
Silent wind not blowing
Pixels of blank pages
The absence of light
The absence of day
The presence of vacuum
The time between here
        and now
Sounds
Words
Spoken.

Missing

Do you see this?
Of course not.
   isn't there.

Disney World

Even in Disney World
Every day's the same
Only the tourists change
Micky and Goofy
Change insides frequently
For after five thousand boat rides
Adventureland isn't an
Fantasyland loses its
Tomorrowland has one too many yesterdays
And nobody really lives in Epcot
    (despite the name).

So Far

So far
on my job
I have been told
to work slower
    socialize more
    look busy
    not work overtime
    get things done
    save paper
    copy everything
    etc.

I don't get paid enough for this.

Pegasus

Pegasus
old prom date
who jerked drugstore sodas in Arizona
has disappeared
into time's sea
even the soda fountain is gone
like Arizona's ocean
only the beach remains
I remember her
but she is gone
flown over the moon
on white wings
young and graceful
to never-never land
never to return
Still
like youth
she haunts me
like all missed chances
like all myths
when we believed what the gods said
when we believed
So
my flying horse
of teenage dreams
wherever you are
I wish you well
and wonder
if you remember me
as some lost
misguided
Apollo.

Orange Sunrise

Orange sunrise over Atlanta
Near the shortest day
First freeze of the fall
As trees sprout bells and balls
Tis the season to be cold
No ice yet, but soon
Flowers moved in, coats out
The TV yells "buy, buy"
Brokers say "sell, sell"
Preacher calls "give, give"
Babies cry "why, why"
Something is dying here
Like a pansy in the snow.

In Middle Age

In middle age
the world cools
wives forbid hot women
so ends the chase
jobs become jobs
not career prospects
novelty becomes impossible
dreams get stale
you have what you have
you are what you are
and if the blood is slower
it is not you becoming older
it is a world gone cold.

The Players

The players have arrived
and methinks they brought their elephants
to catch the conscience of a king
or commoner, any little shift
requires an elephant or two
the play is not the thing
and those who strut and fret
their hour upon the stage
do not earn back the nut
to be or not to be a writer of TV
some Ben is writing TV ads
a Will is into films
the stuff that dreams are made on
and our little lives are rounded
with a sleep.

Dear Sir

The answer to your question
No
You can't
You won't
It's not allowed
It's immoral
It's illegal
It's not the custom
Mother wouldn't like it
Somebody might object
It might corrupt the kids
It's offensive
It's obscene
It's not polite
And I wouldn't like it

So don't you dare
Or I'll blow your fucking brains out
With my god-dammed thirty-eight.

Anniversary 5

Five years
Now, slaves of Elizabeth
gone the dashing dramatist
no longer noble nutritionist
we are changers of diapers
pillows for sleepy heads
sleep and sanity have escaped
gone south for the duration
but, somehow
we endure
holding on
when time is gone
surviving for something
almost forgotten
but never gone
something that
bound us together
five years ago
and binds us still.

Volcanic Ash

Driving into evening fire
Cresting the hill
Atlanta burns like Sherman returned
Beyond, earth's ashes glow
I watch the embers of the world
Slowly fade to black.

Milk Cartons

The silent door
answers the knock

Visions of fat cops
in triplicate
dance in my head

Missing heartaches
on milk cartons.

The Babysitter's Door

The silent door
answers my knock
darkness fills the windows
I pound again
visions of fat cops
in triplicate
dance in my head
missing heartaches
on milk cartons
a memory of curls
not her
not me
not knowing
the cyclops peephole
stares me down
I reach for reasons
and begin to wait
as long as necessary.

On the Day

On the day that Ruby shot Oswald
I was thirteen years old
and visiting a friend's dairy farm
I saw a cow moaning over her calf
stiff-legged on the ground
looking through the fence
at eyes big with death
I saw I did not understand
but knew I would see it over and over
until I learned.

The Seven-Month-Old

Her father said she was kidnapped from his truck
when he stopped on the Yellow River Bridge
to help two strangers with car trouble
the police said there were inconsistencies
in what the father said, and searched the river

The Yellow River is small, shallow, muddy, and quiet.

Birdsong

The birdsong does not rhyme
to my distant ears
the leaves have turned gray
and died
I feel my numb hands
as rigor mortis sets in
prematurely
sunset has come early
but the twilight
may be long.

Muffy

Muffy, a cat
has a wide smile
that draws me in
and holds me
fascinated
by the soft hair
and the wet kiss
of the tongue
Petting her
scratching her back
sliding in and out
of the warm fur
feeling her back arch
to meet my strokes
a purr of contentment
come again and again
as my touches and strokes
bring her to the peak
of pussy pleasure
then she curls up
in my arms
the epitome
of satisfaction.

All Around

All around and
By and by
Comes the ceaseless
Dream of doom
Enough is enough
For fatal fears
Gone to graves
Hidden in hills
In the inner
Jumble of January
Keeping the keen
Long and lean
Man and moment
Now in night
On an open
Point of pain
Quietly, it's quite
Real, a refined
Stealth that slides
Through the twilight
Under the unknown
Vine, past very
Wise owls whose
Xenophobia is Xeroxed
Yawing like youth
Zenlike, Zephyrus.

Days

There are twenty-nine days left in the year
Today is the three hundred thirty-seventh day
It's a leap year, so there's an extra day
The world will probably not end this year
At least not in nuclear fire
Though it shows signs of illness
From the ice of glacial overpopulation
But that moves slowly, at least at first
And seems, like AIDS, to spread from south to north
So, baring car crashes and heart attacks
We can probably count on seeing the New Year
And sit there, counting time lost and gained
What was done and left undone
Said and left unsaid, what will be
What might be, what will not be
And the total of the partial sum of life
This day, or any day, can be many things
But always a surprise.

Light

If, in this pause in the jackhammer
I had something significant to say
I would not feel the silence lost
But my mind, like the sky, is empty
The everyday light hiding
The blazing stars beyond.

One Night

One night
and maybe soon

the phone will ring
a death
tears
an unsmiling airplane
as she
or I
to mother
or father
fly
to say words
make arrangements
and cry
ashes, dust
a cold day in July
an empty place
a long goodbye
and then
a fear
of phones
of nights
that cry.

AIDS

Acquired
Immune
Deficiency
Syndrome
Attacks
Hearts
Hardening
Solidifying
Among
Uninfected
Fear.

Cure

I do not think
we need to worry
about overpopulation

In Africa
we see already
the cure administered

AIDS, war, and drought
tribal genocide
when all the elephants are gone

And Sahara
the Nile's source touches
only bleached bones will need more room.

Modern Nursery Rhymes

Jack and Jill went up the hill
To snort a load of powder
Jack blew his crown and never came down
And Jill can't stop her laughter.

Little Miss Muffet, zonked like a Muppet
Smoking her crack all day
A narco came down, slipped the cuffs round
And led Miss Muffet away.

Mary had a little smack
It's color white as snow
And everywhere that Mary went
She sold her ass for dough.

Mistress Mary, cocaine fairy
How does your business grow?
With little Nells to cocks to sell
And needled maids in a row.

I Spend the Day

I spend the day
staring at blank pages
listening to bits of talk
draining from other cubes
I am an employee
I must look busy
even if my work is done
I cannot sit and read
the boss forbids such ease
so I scribble lines of verse
that resemble computer instructions
though probably more clear
and certainly more concise.

A Living

William Carlos Williams
was a doctor
Charles Ives
sold insurance
Lawrence Ferlinghetti
    sells books
Nobody
lives on songs
No matter how
wonderful the tune.

All

The Arab said
To the Israeli
We are all Jews
We are all Germans.

Theatre

Is
       living on the edge of truth
       balancing on the knifepoint of beauty
       assuming the sun won't rise.

Bloody Lines

easy, bloody lines
nothing obtuse
or referential
just sliced veins
raw nerves
guts on the floor

poetry.

A Valentine

A Valentine anniversary
Enclosed, thirty-nine words of love
This is the first
And forever the last
You are my love
Till angels sing of never.

The Frog

The frog I met on the parking lot
Is one more frog soon forgot
He hippityed when he should have hopped
And now that frog is a bunch of glop.

Exploratory Haiku

They opened him up
      took one look and sewed him up
           after seeing no hope.

Reviewing the Year

Reviewing the year
page by page
it's obvious
a lot happened
memories get jolted
by jots on paper
people came and went
events occurred
a meeting here
a dentist there
here a lunch
there a reminder
to buy something
to pay a bill
to fix some door
and in between
each noted moment
the empty white space
of our lives.

Parents

Torturing babies and toddlers
could be a profitable occupation
never socially acceptable, of course
like garbage men
and sewer workers
or undertakers
there is sufficient demand
in most major cities, it seems
only part-time work
in small towns
but since it requires so little training
or skills
most parents
prefer
to do it themselves.

The Mill

When the mill
has ground the bone
and the meal
is shifted out
my grains will bleach
in the dust
indistinguishable
from the battered sand.

Three Good Things about Life

1. It's not your fault you have it
2. It's not overly contagious
3. Eventually it ends.

The Voices

The voices in the other room disturb my thoughts
I listen to the uhs and ahs
and other sounds that lack a sense of sense
Sounds and voices drone, a mindless pile of words
The pain is that the words ring clear and sharp
It is the sense that's muddy, dull, and drear
Like reading minds that slumber and dream
Surreal, sans reason, unrestrained, untamed
Is this the inner life of man, upmumbled
Upjumbled, the thoughtless thoughts, the unsound sound?

The Vase

The vase sat on the shelf
dusty
designed to hold beauty
and life
it stood empty
the hardened clay
developing minute cracks
it wanted use
else one day
a shattering
even as it sat.

Words

              words
            are like
        bricks that you
      stack one on another
    until you have constructed an
  edifice reaching to the gods above.

Come, He Said

Come, he said
under the bush
now is the time
to be woman

Come, she said
over the tree
catch the bird
known to thee

For this is life
under the sun
coming and going
knowing and known
it begins and ends
natal to grave.

Forbidden Sorority Names

Nu Upsilon Nu
Beta Upsilon Mu
Mu Alpha Nu
Gamma Alpha Mu
Lambda Eta Gamma
Beta Eta Delta
Sigma Eta Xi
Alpha Sigma Sigma
Tau Iota Tau

Question

What's on the inside side
of a belly belly button?
Does an innie stick out
and an outie go in?
What's left of whatever was there
when it led from dear old mother to where?
The outside side was cut and clamped,
knotted or tied
Till a baby belly button bloomed
astride our front side
But the inside side was left alone
with the other muscle and bone
So what was there did what it liked,
as we made mudpies or rode our trikes
Leaving me wondering, as gentlemen do,
of kites and skies, of wheres and whys,
Of uncles and hymns, of do or dies,
of belly belly button inside sides.

Villanelle for a Cat

Even the cat is mad at me
And stares me down with hungry eye
Because it's feeding time, you see

Because he will not pay his fee
And I'm content to let him lie
Even the cat is mad at me

All I charge for dinner and tea's
A moment's petting on my thigh
Before it's feeding time, you see

But not so low his dignity
To such he will not mollify
Even the cat is mad at me

Soon the case will reach perigee
One of us must eat humble pie
Because it's feeding time, you see

PhD versus pedigree
And I've no need to wonder why
Even the cat is mad at me
Because it's feeding time, you see.

Sonnet

Resigned my job, I did, I did, without
another waiting. Now I sit and stare
at terror's empty eye. And soon, no doubt
they say, fortune will fix her silent glare
upon my grave condition. But why,
I say, should she smile now, when never luck
has found me. I left without a sigh
for empty future's reasons. I was stuck
in ruts and holes not of my digging.
So fates are cast to winds that blow to fair
or foul, not by some deity of rigging,
but thermals, sunspots, Niños off Peru
obey the laws of chance, that send some sailors that dare
safely home, others to the devil's jailors.

Pierced Dreams

Pierced dreams
like balloons
flutter and die
breath escaping
some jagged hole
of backstabber
or leaking shrilly
by pin-prick fate
till flat
on ground
colors that flew
collapse
never again
to sail
the bright skies.

The Turn

Where was the turn?
The road was unmarked
Was it dark or right
Left or light?
I couldn't stay parked
I never learn
The map was outdated
Directions had faded
I'm stopping here
Which is where?
North, South, East, West
From where I stand
Nothing is best
The lay of the land
Offers no clue
To where, or why, or who.

But Fourteen Lines

A sonnet is but fourteen lines, I'm told
Iambic feet with minor amphibrachs
Or other unavoidable or old
Soft variations of truth and facts.
Lines of pentameter of course, so five
Of each iambic feet combine to form
A single line. Now rhymes a pattern strive
To make, says the established norm.
Just alternate the lines in groups of four
And end with final syllables the same
And then the last two lines, and never more
Should final thought a sound give name
So there you have a sonnet writ, in sum
It's now the time to simply smile, by gum.

He and I

The unknown Portuguese sailor
whose portrait hangs on my wall
was visiting Boston on a sunny day
and happened to catch an artist's eye
a moment's repose
as pastels flew
then he was gone
to crowds or sea or foreign land
then an artist's gift to a friend
my marriage to her
and the Iberian brown eyes
from the slightly tilted head
stare down at those below
leaving us to wonder, he and I
what sees or is seen
and where and why
the eyes, the eyes, the eyes.

What If

What if
I never
why
      a wage
wind blows
      wind blows
stretch time
      hangs
wait   what
      want
to be
      to be
to be what
      why
      when
then   how
where
if not
what
      streets
            empty buildings
shame
      soft
            useless
to be
      to be
a job to be
      a job
to be
      to do
            to earn
so false
      so true

respect
self   others
    not cry
is why
    want
    to be
        to be
some
    thing
        body
            one
who made
        it
    did
        it
    am
        it
what
    what
        what
what if
    not then
or never
    ever
again
    to be
    to be
    to be
    to be

I see.

Brahma Says

Brahma says
    not feeling
        is good
    not knowing
        is better
    not being
        is best
Nirvana is
    the peace
        of not caring
Enlightenment
    is seeing
        the illusion
            is not real
We
    are not
        real
So it doesn't
    matter
what we feel
    know
    are
So why do it?

It only hurts.

Wandering

Wandering
    town to town
    place to place

Going home
>   to new address
>   unknown faces
Phone number
>   in pocket
>   not mind
Seeded garden
>   long past
>   long gone.

Take a Man

If you take a man
and squeeze him
till the blood runs
out his mouth
you can see what you've done
it can be reported
in the *Times* or the *Sun*
not every vise however
is such cold steel
nor does blood
so often flow.
In this junkyard
the body press
calls forth the silent scream
of worn-out Ramblers
or lost Esprit
but the compressed hulks
keep moving
in the traffic flow
rusted tears staining the grill
gas gage stuck on low
It's not a way to go.

Writers

The famous Southern poet
now old, writes, they say
two hours a day
the jockey-turned-mystery
writer goes for six
on yellow legal pads
while staring at the sea
the Hollywood female
of scandal/romance fame
went for ten or twenty
in bursts of weeks
till done or exhausted
(she's dead)

There are those
who live to write
and those
who write to live
and many
somewhere in between

But how much is said
and how much worth saying
and who says it best
is not an hours test.

Writing

Writing is easy
Selling is hard
Xeroxes and stamps
S.A.S.E., rejection slips
Blood, sweat, tears
Faceless names
Nameless faces
"We regret to inform . . ."
"There were many considerations"
"We received 2947 submissions"
"Please keep us in mind"
"We are no longer reading . . ."
"Return to sender, delivery refused"

Writing is easy
Selling is hard.

For Real

There is for real a moon called blue
And chickens once had teeth
And hell, from what men say, then do
Must freeze each quarter hour

If these be true, then love can too
A thing not out of reach
So start anew just me and you
And ecstasy we'll teach.

By the Time

By the time the call comes
no one will answer
no one will be left
just a shuck of dry-year corn
we have a job for you
they will want to say
but it will be too late
the man will be gone
something may pick up the phone
maybe even say yes
hollow yes, echo yes, empty yes
yes too late, after no no no no
"He who lives on hope dies farting"
if no then no why no so no
no, no, no, no, no
the silent telephone
the empty mailbox
the dry days months years
even the Arizona frogs
who dormant go till water
or desert seeds that lie years till rain
if no rain, if no water, if no
then one day the limit will pass
no yes then will bloom the dry seed
no yes then will stir the empty egg
no yes then will save the gone soul
no yes then will be answered
by more than hollow man
by more than echo no.

To Write

To write
you have
to think

That makes
it hard

To write
you have
to feel

That makes
it hurt

To write
you have
to know

That makes
it impossible.

Church

Through the glass darkly I stare
Far away a bell tolls
The sound is silence
Someone cries an empty tear

The churches are full
      of empty people

Lo, I am with you
      not peace but a sword

The stained glass bleeds
The choir is hired
Ah, look at all the lonely
From here they do come from.

Good Sense

Nonsense rhymes with horsesense
And horsesense is oxymoronic
So horsesense is nonsense
But not recipricalic
For nonsense can make sense
An amazing, wonderful trick
Which makes no sense
at all.

Dear God

Dear God
    Thank you for everything you have given us
    Give us wisdom and knowledge
        health and strength
        understanding and humility
    Bless Mom and Dad and Donna
        Peter Craig, Scott Heumann, Pam Maddox
        Doug Seitz, Jane Berndt, Mana Covington
        Peggy Olin, Tom Chimawong, Lenelle Davis
        David Carter, Chris Alexander, Amy Smith
        Bill Gilliland, Barbara Sandacz, Roberta Smith
        Beverly and Bob Pevitts, Kaarin Johnston
        and all my friends and enemies
    Lead us and guide us and help us
        to stay in thy will
    We pray for Kelsy Koonce, heal her
        and help her sing again

    Help us with our writing and music
        our studies and relationships with other people
    Forgive all our sins
    Lead us in all we say and do
    Keep us healthy and alive
    Thank you for Kathy and all her love and care
    We pray in Jesus's name
        Because we love him
Amen.

Villanelle

I do not want to write a villanelle
They're just too hard, too much a rhyming trick
I wish that I could somehow break their spell

Some poets can dash them off pell-mell
I waddle on through words molasses thick
I do not want to write a villanelle

The rhymes have but a two-tone knell
That rings like childish, obscene limerick
I wish that I could somehow break their spell

A bad one smells like long-dead mackerel
A good one reads like formal rhetoric
I do not want to write a villanelle

Obsessed by this, a literary muscatel
A maverick, love-sick, drunken lunatic
I wish that I could somehow break their spell

I'm in a kind of minor poet's hell
To think that this would be my bailiwick
I do not want to write a villanelle
I wish that I could somehow break their spell.

Ulcer

I have an ulcer up my ass
the bloody thing won't die
So silver nitrate gets applied
(isn't that the stuff on film?)
My ass could take a picture now
of pitch-dark colon wall
Developing the ugly thing
is a neater trick, however
So Eastman Kodak or Polaroid
get on the stick, you guys
What's needed here, I'm sad to say
is instamatic assfilm.

Heavy Lines

Light verse
weighs about
three words per ounce

Serious verse
on the other hand
gets about
seven words
to a pound

And Ezra Pound
will break the scales
at four words
to the ton.

Verse

Playing with rhyme takes time
There's near and false, sight and true
Internal, external, ten dollar, two for a dime
So much moon, June, balloon it makes you blue
It's easy to rhyme hope, mope, and dope
But translunar, sea schooner, and piano tuner
Take pushing and twisting a line to cope
With such almost and nearly and why didn't I sooner
Think of that. But hardest of all
(it's made me bald) is avoiding the nursery
Rhyme tune. It drives one up the wall
To hit rhyme after rhyme, in verse after versery
Line after line, a Mother Goose loose
Off her caboose, on the juice, short a deuce
Should hang by the noose, I have no more use
For such overdone, bad as a pun, too long in the sun
Stun like a gun, makes your bowels run, rhyme.

Doing Sit-ups

Doing sit-ups
on the floor
in the morning
my cat watches me
thinking
he owns
a curious
human.

Lucky 7 (Anniversary 1993)

7, lucky 7, years
4 as 2, 3 as 3
4 and 3, even and odd
square and triangle
mismatches mathematically fitting
geometry of wonder
wondering, enduring, surviving
tears, time, toil
little joy and her little toys
tempering each other
huddled against the cold
I love you, you love me
we're a happy family
testing time together
you and I and she
2, now 3, against eternity.

Getting Dressed

My daughter believes
that getting dressed
on winter mornings
does not require
waking up.

Dear Elizabeth

Mommy, as usual, was worried
and asked me to explain something.
She was afraid one day you would read
a play or poem I wrote
that said something not nice
about daughters, or babies, or being a daddy
and think I meant you
and think I didn't love you.

Mommy doesn't always understand about writing
how it takes parts of things
of events, of people, of feelings
and puts them together in new ways
that are part me, part not me,
some things added, and a lot left out.
Sometimes it's the love part that gets left out.

Sometimes it isn't about me, or you, at all.
There is one play Mommy thinks is about her
that talks about a daughter in a not-nice way
It was written even before you were conceived.

So, if you ever read anything I wrote
about little girls or babies or parents
and think it's not nice, remember
The love part got left out.

But in our lives, between me and you,
the love part
never gets left out.
I did, do, and will
love you

with every bit of love I've got.
Love,
Daddy.

Octagon

Eight years, an octagon of time
multisided, alternating corners and straights
too rough to be a circle of love
the gold ring, smooth and polished
is the target, not the state

Physicists say the three-body problem is insolvable
so we two planets and a satellite
spin around each other
in unpredictable orbits
approaching the order of chaos
held together by the gravity of love

Newton is out the window, eating oranges
no orbit is as calculated
we wobble through the universe
three wave/packets exchanging heart-red gravitons
eight years into eternity
outward bound together.

Yesterday

Yesterday
my daughter asked me
what I wanted to be
when I grew up
I told her
I want to be
a writer.

New Year's Day, 1995

Reading avant-garde poetry
listening to my father die
imagining letters
made by drying rain
on the roof below
waiting for the football game.

Combing My Daughter's Hair

My daughter's hair
is long, blond, and tangled
Every morning
it's brush, brush, brush, brush
Until I gleam
      from the polish of its touch.

The Nude

The oil painting
over my desk
of the nude girl
is a memory
of my father

In his last days
amid the chemo
and radiation
he hung her
by his bedside
an unfather—
unpreacher—act

After his death
she came to me
and on my wall
looks down
with some
paternal secret
important, yes
meaningful, but
a secret
I cannot read
in the curves
and smile
he chose to view
as his life ebbed
and went away.

No Iambic

No iambic
pentameter
quatrain, sonnet
a b a b
c c d d
for me, oh no
I count sylla.

NRA

National Recovery Administration
National Rifle Association
Oh god that NRA stood for
Not Really Anything.

Rocks and Leaves

My daughter
collects leaves
and rocks

they're free
which matters
when you're five

the leaves
are crayon red
yellow, orange

the rocks
are, well
rocks

the leaves
scattered
on a table

in time
become brown
and crumble

the rocks
remain
rocks.

1986-1995

Nine-tenths of a decade
somewhat short of a milestone
hardly worth the notice
just another year that passed
same job, same house, same wife
a death here and there, true
an old guitar, some pictures, some metal files
DramaPlay, Sex and Violence, Disney World
for the kid, new school, baptism, traffic jams
for the wife, operations, college teaching
just life passing by
nothing worth mentioning
just hanging in there
just hanging on
to you.

Daddy? (1)

Daddy, why are you always so sad?

Because I am waiting for the other shoe to drop
for the accident, disease, the tragedy
that will tear us apart
maybe I'll get sick again, or have a heart attack
or slip on one of the toys you leave on the floor
and be crippled for life
maybe I'll get cancer like my father did
or go away on a trip and lose your love
like my father did with his daughter
during his pilgrimage to the holy land
maybe Mommy will have a stroke
or get so depressed she will leave me
or us or just not cope anymore
And maybe you will get sick, like I did
as a child, or fall off one of those
high places you are always climbing on
and crack your skull or choke
or get run over or get kidnapped or . . .

So, I am sad that we may be torn apart
or one of us die or, perhaps worse, one of us
end up crippled and bitter, run out of hugs and kisses
so we become no longer a family
three people loving each other
So every time I see you climb on a counter
or leave a pen on the floor or stand on the tub
every time Mommy eats too much
or has to change medicine
or stays up late doing crafts
every time I miss my exercise
or get narrowly missed by another car

every time you don't do what I ask you to do
because you know better
or know how to do it yourself
or know it won't happen to you
I think of my long days in the hospitals
of three young men who drove under trucks
and had their heads cut off
of my friend's mother who died drooling
in a rest home in her forties of a stroke
of Scott H. and Jim G., who had or have AIDS
of Deborah I. and her two fatherless children
of my own father and how we loved him
but didn't like him after we grew up
and it makes me very, very sad.

Daddy? (2)

Daddy, why are you always so sad?

Do I seem that way, my darling?
Maybe I am. I'm sorry
I don't mean to be sad
I guess I'm just waiting
      for another shoe to drop
      another dream to end
      another day to pass
          into eternity
          for no reason
I'm sad that the house is so messy
      that you don't always listen to me
      that I don't have time to play with you
          as much as you want
I'm sad my job is boring and frustrating
      and not what I wanted to do
          with my life
I'm sad my toes and knees and jaw and hands
          hurt so much
      that I never get enough exercise
      and am tired all the time
I'm sad I was sick so much as a boy
      and don't know the childhood games
          you want to play
I'm sad I don't believe everything I used to
      and everything seems so uncertain now
I'm sad Mommy is fat and depressed
      and has to take psychoactive drugs
      and spends all her time on crafts
      instead of helping me clean the house
      or fix the meals
      or get you dressed

I am sad I am getting old and you
      are still so young
I am sad because I am scared
      I will get sick again
      or you will get sick
          like I did
      or one of us will be hurt
          or killed in the Atlanta traffic
      or I will have a heart attack
      or Mommy will have a stroke
      or you will fall and hurt yourself
          forever
I am afraid I will end up alone again
      with only pictures and memories
      that you will leave me
      or I will die and leave you
      and you will be very sad
I guess I am sad because I am alive
      and see all the sadness
      that might come to you
          or me
And that makes me sad.

To Whom It May Concern

To whom it may concern
Some dreams to remember me by
Broadway marque, my name in black letters
(I made two weeks off-Broadway, non-equity)
Two women in the same bed, hot to trot
(I had a good wife and a sweet daughter)
Walking, tan and lean, into the Arizona sunset
(I had arthritis, was overweight, and stayed in Georgia)
It was the dreams that killed me.

Pretending to Nap

I play with my daughter
by pretending to nap
while she piles dolls around me
and paints makeup on my face
it makes her happy
and lets me think
but she is disappointed
when I do not laugh
in surprise
when I wake
she wonders if I ever laugh
I say "Sometimes"
she says once a year
maybe
and she is right
I guess I am
a better father
asleep.

You See

At rise, we don't see
Well, what did you . . .
I could have told . . .
It's not like . . .
On the other hand
There is no . . .
We have no . . .
That's just the way . . .
You see?

With 10 Words

With 10 words
      the world could change forever or at least a while
with 9 words
      a man might die, or perhaps learn to live
with 8 words
      the sun may set or rise in glory
with 7
      a baby cries alone in the night
with 6
      a wind blows from the north
with 5
      a woman kisses her lover
with 4
      the soft rain falls
with 3
      a smile appears
with 2
      grass grows
with 1
      laughter

but I have no words.

I Need Time

I need time
words do not grow on paper
without sun and shade
water and soil
winter and summer
the garden needs tending
and fallow seasons
deep plowing
observant eyes
and time
to grow.

For Us All

The mountains do not cry
brooks do not sob
but I can sit
by the stream
and weep
for us all.

Ache

My shoulders hurt
stress
the doctor says
boss
riding my back
really
killing me slowly
stupid.

Something Useful

I could be doing something useful
going swimming
taking my daughter's picture
mailing scripts
reading my father's sermons
instead
of sitting in an office cubicle
waiting
for a supervisor to read her email
but no,
employment is by the hour
not
by the job
so
I waste
life.

When I Was Young

When I was young
    alone in my bachelor pad
        I dreamed (fantasized?)
            of living with a woman

When I was older
    married and settled
        I dreamed (fantasized?)
            of having many women

Now I am old
    husband, father
        I dream (fantasize?)
            of being alone.

Low Gear

My brain is in low
towing a load
up a mountain grade
and losing traction.

I Want Silence

I want silence
empty space
a desert at night
the noise of owl wings
and snakes
the glare of
       the Crab Nebula
       and Polaris
the gossip of
       cosmic rays
       and neutrinos
the traffic of
       brown cougar
       and black bear
to keep me company
       and bring me
       loneliness
again.

At Five

My daughter, at five
is afraid to go to sleep
for fear of monsters
stalking the night

I, at forty-five
crave the release of sleep
from the fear of monsters
stalking the day.

Screen Saver

The computer screen-saver
of geometric shapes
and ever-changing hues
supposedly preserves
the phosphorescent screen
from photoelectric overstimulation
resulting in images
burned into the screen
leaving electronic ghosts
persistent photon illusions

I, on the other hand
have persistent illusions
under-stimulation
and false images
of a symmetric life
and no savior
in sight.

The Beach

The beach
where I lived
as a boy
has been
washed away
by a hurricane
the shifting sand
of my youth
is now at sea
drifting with the tide
making me feel
right at home.

Divide

Standing on the Continental Divide
watching the future flow away
in one direction or another
wondering on which side
my drop of life will fall.

The Office

Sterile green cubicle
filled by babbling voices
and white noise
roofless, doorless, colorless
inhabited by personnel
who used to be people.

In Two Days

In two days
Elizabeth will be six
In twenty-nine days
I will be forty-six
Old enough
to add and subtract
the days and years
to carry over
and cipher
the remainder.

November One

November One, Nineteen Ninety-six
Dead in stagnant water
Only a memory of a breeze
      in my sails
Ship in disarray
Crew pulling one rope
      in two directions
Motionless, rudderless
At the mercy of a current
      going nowhere
Drifting into the silence
      of a waveless sea.

October 13, 1996

On October 13, 1996
my daughter
lost her first baby tooth
three days later
I became
Forty-six years
long in the tooth

Looking a horse
in the mouth
is rude
but informative

My daughter
danced with delight
at this evidence
of her maturing
my birthday was more somber
but
she is growing up
and
I am growing old.

No Bananas

Yes, we have no bananas
No, I am not awake

It's hard to write poetry
      with your eyes closed
           and your mind shut

Is white noise always white

or is there off-white noise
that tells off-color jokes
and paints faces red
among those with colorless lives

And what of black noise
does it have soul to sing the blues
does it rock and roll in a red dress
when played to a white heat

Is there a rainbow of sounds
with a pot of gold at the end
for anyone spotless and pure at heart
arrayed in iridescence
refracting sunlight
into life?

Little Muse

Where oh where has my little muse flown
oh where or where can she be
with her easy rhymes
and quick dialogue
oh where oh where can she be

With her sexy bare breasts
and witty blond hair
oh where on where has she gone
over the rainbow and through the woods
oh where oh where can she be?

Don't Read This

"Don't Read This"
flashes three times a second
on my computer screen
a command
like most office instructions
impossible to follow.

Ten (Anniversary 1996)

Has it been ten years?
A decade?
Since our thanksgiving
the day after
Are we three honeymoons
two dwellings
and one child
down the road already?
Yes, I guess we are
The scars on your tummy
and breast
like the ache in my joints
testify
to events, to ordeals
to the toll we paid
to cross
all those bridges
And Elizabeth stands
as witness
to union, to time, to family
Ten years
Time and furniture
are heaped around us
testament to our passing

from children to parents
from lovers to spouses
from friends to partners
from love to love.

Still Standing

Are we still standing?
Sometimes I am not so sure
the body-blows accumulate
vision turns gray
and I stagger to you
hoping you too
are still standing.

Sherlock Holmes

Sherlock Holmes
when devoid of mysteries
seeing gray sameness
roll in like London fog
occasionally escaped
courtesy of cocaine
which illustrates
the difference between
genius and wisdom
but explains the temptation
wrestled with
by those behind
gray-walled cubicles
doing changeless tasks
devoid of mysteries.

The Faces

The faces
        that used to be young
are now getting old
blonds bleached
        to have more fun
now fight gray roots
eyes have character
        not sparkle
windblown skin, not hair
        tanned, not tan
we dress too well
        see too much
                feel too little
and only endure
like the rocks
we resemble.

Write Anything

Write anything
keep the hand moving
pray the brain hasn't died
yet
RIP
    Here lies a wasted mind
    Killed by boredom
        bureaucracy
        and bad timing
    Underlying diseases
        included extreme introversion
        judgmental rearing
        and lack of socialization
    complicated by
        inhibitions
        innocence
        and lack of confidence
    brought on by
        childhood illness
        dysfunctional family
        and being different
Services will be scheduled
as soon as the body
stops breathing.

Once Upon A Time

Once upon a time
a long, long time ago
maybe even a whole week ago
in a land far, far away
too far to walk to
in less than an hour
there lived a little girl
who was really a princess
but of course, nobody knew that
not even her parents
who only thought
she was real special
Anyway, this little girl
being six years old
knew everything
or at least thought she did
though she wasn't sure
what number came
after googooplus
or how to make a Z
without getting it backwards
but she could find
the Cartoon Network
by herself
and pour her own milk
if the carton wasn't too full
and get dressed by herself
if there weren't too many buttons
The only reason
she didn't do all the cooking herself
was that she wasn't allowed
to turn on the stove
and she thought she could drive a car

except she didn't have a license
This special little princess
had lots of sisters
who were all really dolls
so she lived alone
with her parents
who weren't much fun
always working or cooking or cleaning
    or writing plays or making crafts
    or applying for jobs or talking on the phone
She tried to invite friends over to play
but her mommy had to ask their mommy
and the mommies could never work things out
as easily as the kids could have
so lots of times she ended up alone
with her dolls and toys and TV
    and books and computer and keyboard
or she had to go with her parents
shopping or to parties or to restaurants
that didn't even give away balloons
So the little girl had to go to school
    and the after-school program
    and church on Sunday
    and dance class
    and art class
    and gymnastics
    and never had time
        to watch all thirty-six episodes
        of Scooby Doo
        or Garfield
        or the Flintstones
        and almost never got to see
            the Jetsons
        because it was on
            after eight at night

        and she had homework to do
        (though her parents did help
        because sometimes she had trouble
        even though she was very smart)
        and baths to take and teeth to brush and floss
        and it all took so much time
        and she was supposed to be asleep
        by nine o'clock on school nights
So anyway, this tall, beautiful princess
thinking about all these things
decided to see if she could grow up
while no one was looking
and see if anybody would notice
so she did, but nobody paid any mind
So, after a while, she went back
to being a little girl
which, you must admit,
was the princess thing to do.

Another Christmas

I'm not ready for another Christmas
It's not the shopping I mind
It's the fun, the glowing memories
I'm supposed to create
Food, family, goodwill toward everybody
Well, the food makes me fat
My family drives me up a wall
And goodwill is now a tax-deductible donation
Made through imitation Santas from Laos
On every street corner, bell and ho-ho-ho in hand

I want to kiss my daughter
On Christmas morning
Not pick up wrapping paper

Have my wife and mother
Watch the parade on TV
Instead of having me mediate
Between family traditions
It's a holiday
Something to do with love
And giving me something
Besides a hard time.

Doggerel

Doggerel
all I can think of
is doggerel
where oh where
has my doggerel gone
how much is that doggerel
in the window
that doggerel won't hunt
or scan or bark or bite
his bark is worse
than his bite
and he won't bite
unless you tease him
he's a good doggerel
aren't you, boy?

Scars

The scars mark off the years
like scratches on a prison wall
circumcision, tonsils, adenoids
muscle biopsies, acne
super-pubic catheter, prostate
excised illusions, reconfigured heart
in the end
we die
from too many scars.

Reeling

Reeling like a stunned fighter
blinded by sweat and blood
crouched over, ducking on instinct
the stressed jab
the sickening thud
the disbelieving leather
wary of the hammer hook
the fated cross
the unexpected blow
you know is coming
knowing there is no bell.

Davis Family, 1997

Was it the worst year ever?
So much pain, anger.

Reeling like a stunned fighter
blinded by sweat and blood,
crouched over, ducking on instinct

the stressing jab
the sickening thud
the disabling leather,
wary of the knockout hook
the fated cross
the unexpected low blow,
despairing of the bell
but standing
somewhere beyond reason.

Are we still standing?
Weak and nearly beaten
but standing,
grasping our agony
with each other,
reassembling the shards
of our senses and life
with the glue of pain
tears, and love.
If necessary,
on hands and knees
with our heart blood.

When I Was Young

When I was young
I wore soft shoes
and learned to walk
almost soundlessly
on all but the driest leaves

Now I am old
I wear soft shoes
and walk quietly
having spent a life
making no sound.

Senior Prom

My date to the Senior Prom
forever lithe eighteen in memory
must be pushing fifty now
and wondering
whatever became of me
and if anyone
will remember us
when we are gone.

I Am

I am not depressed
depression is caused
by chemicals
playing teeter-totter
in the brain

I am sad
sadness is caused
by life
teetering on the edge
or tottering off
to old age

I am not depressed
I am sad.

Contemplating Oceans

Contemplating oceans
Juggling words
Poetry.

The Dead Horse

The dead horse
was carried
by the tow truck
through the rain
to wherever
horses go
when they die.

Daddy? (3)

My daughter keeps asking me
why
I am always
sad
Do I tell her
because
my health is shot
my career is in the toilet
her dyslexia and ADD
are breaking my writer's heart
and federal employee wallet
her seriously overweight mother
is showing signs of mental instability
and my playwriting
my best hope of salvation
is turning into a purgatory
of workshops and readings
No
I smile
and say
what makes you think
I'm sad?

Initialisms

If CDC CIOs
met with
CBOs and NGOs
to discuss
HIV and HCWs
would anybody
CARE?

Tired

I wake up tired
little cat feet
walking on my mind
seeing through
an old prescription
wondering if
the haze
will ever
lift?

Tidy Widerman

Where have you gone Tidy Widerman
disappeared like Sunday closing time
to older days of dinosaurs and Desilu
Camelot and Clarabell
into sagas and bedtime stories
sung for seven-year-olds
sparks of ancient campfires
when huddled 'round the TV
for protection from wild beasts
we bravely grabbed our bagless books
and faced the daunting day.

Elizabeth's Pictures

In my office
pictures
form years
of little faces
getting wiser
all the time.

The Ghost Moon

The ghost moon rises
over the morning highway
The green spider floats over the mailbox
      on silent strings
The hazes oppress Atlanta, blurring
      city from town
Mornings are no longer new beginnings
      but faded memories
        of yesteryears' dreams.

Call the Time

Call the time
the fevered husk
force aged
by heat and pressure
cured beyond cure
wrinkled within
old before
and past
its time.

Better

When I was young
life was hard
but I thought
it will get better

Now I am old
life is hard
now
I know better.

Every Time

Every time I think of you
Lying, a babe, in my arms
I get all squishy inside
Zestfully, I remember
All the days you grew
Before my eyes
Even now, far too big
To hold, you are what I
Hold in my heart.

For the Long Haul

Did the paired mules
in the mule teams
count the slow steps
from water hole
to water hole
on the long haul
to Death Valley
or were they content
paired and harnessed
to plod together
to wherever
the sun led?

Twelve years paired
on our long haul
plodding through
spots low and high
scenery blurs
cools springs are mirages
green mountains, dreams
only the endless
sun is real
but your shoulder
is touching mine
your voice is
in my ear
we are together
and if this is all
it is not
a wasted trip.

Kure Beach Terns

Stiff wind out of the north
Too cool for swimming
but fine for hovering
imitating the fishermen on the pier
we toss bits of bread aloft
and are suddenly swarmed
by what my daughter
thinks are seagulls
riding the wind
at arm's length
before our faces
"Toss it up!" I yell
as we stare at motionless wings
just beyond reach
black heads with white bodies
stacked on each layer of air
instantly shifting the few inches
to our errant throws
to gulp our offering
to their courage
to come so near
the dangerous tourists
visiting their sandy domain
it is a miracle of aerobatics
catching in waiting beak
a crust heaved skyward
quicker than I can blink
They surround us now
tens, dozens, scores
almost touching wings
in a formation no human fliers
would dare attempt
I have held hawks

uplifted on my arm
and had pigeons peck seeds
inches from my feet
but never before
have I stood
beside a bird in flight
hanging unmoving before me
no fear in its eyes
calmly treading air
until my bit of bread
found its place
in the flock
My daughter laughs
and I do too
tearing bread into bites
for hungry terns
who fill us with delight.

If I Do Not Cry

If I do not cry
it is not for no reason
If reasons were tears
logic says my eyes would drown
weeping blur my sight
of the cold, clear reasons
I should cry.

Visiting

Visiting places I lived long ago
my father's home
my childhood beach
I expected them to change
to be less than my memory
smaller and shabbier than
my child's protected view
and they were
What was not expected
was that those left behind
still saw their homes
with children's eyes.

And Will We Go

And will we go again
where terns pose in midair
for pictures and bits of bread
or where old farmers
blood kin
cling to land and life
long past their time
will we go again
to past places
and old memories
will we go
where we have been
will we
go
again.

For My Daughter

For my daughter,
Life is getting less poetic
there are no odes to braces
dyslexia does not rhyme
with anything attractive
being nine in 1999
must be like 666
and other unfortunate numbers
occupational therapy
does not have the sound
of ballet classes
being cute is over
and it's hard to be pretty
after inheriting
your mother's tummy
and your poor parents
girding themselves to discuss sex
have no answers to why
kids become mass murderers
of kids
or why grownups
would shoot little Jewish kids
or their own kids
another innocence
is being lost
the warm blanket
that Mommy and Daddy
can take care of me
is unraveling too soon
to face third grade
in these days
requires a different courage
steeling her eyes
glistening in mine.

Rage

Road rage, air rage, job rage, school rage, rage rage
machine guns chatter like gossip around the water cooler
shotguns blow like tires running over nails
assume every teenager has a thirty-eight
every little old lady a forty-five
hate groups and gangs, sheets and trench coats
uniform of the day
is fear and rage.

I Love You More

I love you more
than there are stars
she said to me
an eight-year-old's
attempt at poetry
worried I was growing old
at forty-eight
when do you plan to die?
she asked, as if a man
controlled that date
and then she pointed out to me
each item in her room
by which she could
remember me
ever the good daddy
I calmed her fears
and said I planned to be
around for years
until she was grown
and on her own at least
and eased her off to sleep
cuddling her blankie

between two large dolls
Lydia and Louise
but fathers lie
out of full hearts
and I have no more claim
on tomorrow than anyone
Elizabeth, I will try
to live forever
to kiss your child
or cheer your fate
but if I do not
know forever
my love will.

When the Haze

When the haze accumulates
making it hard to breathe
my mind tightens up
like my chest
I get afraid to walk
or swim or even go out
or write, or think
or even read
slow motion of wasted time
solitaire or sleep
becalmed in the thick air
yawning at the world
wavering in the smog
poisoning my mind
no way to win
in this modern world.

Rust

Trying to write out the rust
I almost fall asleep
bad air and women
who won't go to sleep
an office where appearance counts
more than work does
leave almost nothing of me
or for me
fevers have burned me out
an empty shell of clichés
a government bureaucrat
doing nothing
for forty thousand
and wanting a raise.

Tongue Twister

If Peter Piper picked a peck of pickled peppers
and sold them to the silly Sally
who sells seashells by the seashore
for a penny apiece in price
could he afford to purchase
a pumpkin from Peter the Pumpkin Eater
for the sixth sick sheik
whose sixth sheep is sick
and bit Mary's little lamb
leaving little doubt
what it was all about.

Holding On (Anniversary 1999)

Just when you think
it can't get any worse
it does
and we grab on
to each other
as the stormy waves
plunge us down
to another low
Like sailors in a gale
we search for handholds
one hand for ourselves
one hand for each other
so we're not swept away.

Thirteen years into this voyage
We've weathered our share of storms
the rigging is frayed
the sails worn
but the hull is sound
and the mast is strong
so we sail on
calm sea or high water
shipmates forever
holding on.

The Day after Thanksgiving, 2000

Fourteen years
Double sevens
How lucky can you get.

Come, grow old
and decrepit
with me
the best
and worst
is yet to be.

I'll match you pill for pill
scar for scar
my RA, ostheo, BPH, reflux
against your BP, diabetes, ADD, hormones.

Will we have another fourteen years?
Get to see E in cap and gown
and wedding dress?
Kiss her from our wheelchairs?
Know we hung on long enough
to grow her up?

I cannot ask that question.
Tomorrow is not mine.
What I have is today
and what I have to do today
is all I can handle.
I have to love you
take care of E
and do the laundry.
Everything else is optional.

So, as life gets whittled down
to heartwood,
You have my heart,
which is about all that's left.
Other parts could go at any time.

But when my legs can no longer walk
and my hands no longer feel
my heart will beat for you
as long as life
is real.

Dancing with My Daughter

Dancing with my daughter at her teacher's wedding
was complicated
beyond the fact that neither of us really knows how to dance
and were mostly just swaying to the music
while the wedding party jigged and jived barefoot on the church lawn
and beyond the lingering remnants of my Baptist anti-dance raising
by the effect of a ten-year-old in a thirteen-year-old's body
who has seen too many TV shows and has a bad Electra complex
trying to attach herself like I was her boyfriend instead of her father
catching me between wanting to hold my little girl
and having the proper fatherly attitude toward this new young woman
sprouting on fast forward toward adolescence
leaving me rushing to adjust to each new phase
that seems to come and go
before I realize that she has danced away from me again.

Three Problems

There are three problems with my job
besides the usual not enough pay
and takes too much time and attention
the first is that when I do have some downtime
I cannot read what I want
but have to at least look like I am working
even if that means checking the CNN website for the fifth time today
the second is that I have to, working or not,
stay at my terminal, wasting away from lack of motion
feeling the joints stiffen and the muscles slack
even as I sit hunched over before the monitor eye
the third is that I end up hiring a teenager
to take my daughter to the zoo or the movies
so that at least one of us gets to go
so that at least one of us gets to experience her childhood
I hate this job.

My Right Wrist

My right wrist is so sore
I have switched my mouse
to the left side of the keyboard
and am learning how to left-hand it
this is life in the computer age
of convenience and soft living
where we pay new and different prices
for being in the electronic age
and learn to ache in whole new ways.

Holding

The first time I held my daughter
hours old and half an arm long
like most new fathers
I was afraid I would drop her
Three years later
just home from the hospital
still weak and feeble
I sat in a chair
and they placed her on my lap
toddler now, unsteady
on her own two feet
we were both a little scared
I would not be able to hold her
By seven she was too big to lift
and had to slide into my lap
by nine she was big as a small woman
and almost too heavy to hold
under any circumstances.
Now she sits beside me
and we hold each other
fearing the days coming
when I cannot hold her
and the further day
when she will have to hold me.

Pushing the Envelope

Pushing the envelope
toward to speed of life
the winds buffet
thundering behind us
shaking the thin skin
that protects us
in these upper reaches
jerking the stick
away from our control
blazing engines driving us
wherever we are headed
faster and faster
to punch through
or fall
like forgotten pilots
pictures on a wall
of those who rode the wind
but not the sky.

Youth Elder

My church has a "Youth Elder"
some poor teen each year
selected to be made old
aged by responsibility
rotated from pillar to post
to learn how churches are run
and to speak for those still young
to those grown old
an admirable intent
if oxymoronic
but what we really need
is an "Elder Youth"

an old geezer
selected to be young again
for a year
allowed to run with the pack
to the pizza parties
to flirt and nuzzle
gulp soda and sing songs
and not have to think
about why churches are run.

051701

I have a cold
I am allergic to colds
Sometimes they make me sick
Not just cold sick
or flu sick
but dead sick
hospital sick
long-term disability sick
fevers, chills, atrophy
inflammation of connective tissue
sick of arthritis
that kind of sick
but there is no cure
for the common cold
so I am sick
and afraid.

Thirty-eight Hours

About thirty-eight hours would do it
eight to sleep
eight to work
a couple for commuting
say two a day for meals
(including the cooking)
another two for dressing and bathing,
using the toilet, taking out the trash, etc.
another couple for my daughter,
her homework, reading, talking, playing games,
being the daddy
of course two for my wife
for talking, planning, playing, etc.
(if you know what I mean)
then three hours to read
two more for the TV
one for writing poetry
three for writing plays
and two more for marketing all that stuff
one more for exercise
and one for just goofing off
yeah, thirty-eight hours a day
should be enough
hey, if I gave up sleeping
and working
I could squeeze in
a decent day's living.

My War

My daughter dances
to Sandman
by America
a '70s song
about draft dodgers
in a war
she knows nothing about
except a black slab
in Washington
and a story
about draft numbers
on T-shirts
I told her
to explain why
I was not in
my war.

Great-Grandparents

My mother sent me a picture
of my great-grandparents
and their children
taken about 1890
by a traveling photographer
the parents sit
on chairs moved outside
for the light
in their Sunday best
surrounded by eight children
almost grown
including my grandfather
with a little youth left in him
standing behind in the line
but his parents are old
ancient
my great-grandfather
has eyes that saw the Civil War
through gunpowder and smoke
in more battles
in Northern Virginia
than he cares to remember
but the most ancient
is the mother
like the nightmare of age
she sits in black
more worn than the soldier
staring at the camera
and through its lens
at me and mine
a glint of light
a slice of time

passed down to me
to see what was
and what may be.

051801

Sitting around a Denny's one night
with a bunch of Baptist virgins
of mixed high school age
back in the long ago days
when most high schoolers
actually were virgins
some brave soul asked
what does "horny" mean?
The Senior replied
it's the way guys
and I guess girls too
(oh yes, from the girl next to him)
get when they haven't had sex for awhile
which for most of us
was at least sixteen years
not counting the various solo arts
which left the impression
the Senior was not quite as horny
as the rest of us
but left us unsure
about the girl
but all amazed
we could be horny
and talk about it
at Denny's.

School Pictures

It must be almost summer
all the pictures are coming in
school pictures in T-shirt and jeans
out on the playground
posed before the jungle gym
ballet pictures in leotard
striking the classic pose
of one almost on toe
tap pictures in sequins and spangles
fake guitar and polished shoes
frozen rhythm you can hear
all memories of ten
curls fading to waves
girl fading to near-teen
breast buds and braces
balanced for an instant
on the edge of puberty
still trying to believe
in Santa Clause
and the Easter Bunny
heading for Disney World
while it is still a little real
but knowing, soon
life will change
but not yet
today the pictures came
reminding us forever
of ten.

Splinters

I cry a lot these days
very easily
an old M.A.S.H.
writing a poem
testifying in church
like an old woman
not ashamed of tears
tasting the pain
knowing we all have splinters
just under the skin
working their way out
poking through
at the worst moment
to remind us
of the rough work
that put them there
the days past
when we got things done
knowing the cost
would come later
when what went in
comes tearing out
like a memory
like knowing
like rain.

Drought

The lakes are low
the shoreline is yards from shore,
like dreams from reality
tree stumps that have not seen light
since the dam was born
poke up like old poems
scraping the bottom
of boats as ill-suited
for low water
as men for hard times
other boats are docked on mud
tied to ramps whose floats don't
moored tightly as jobs
The heat of summer is coming
but not rain
Undrinkable words abound,
but not what is needed
no dramatic thunder
or flashes of insight
only hot, dry air
and honestly burning sun.

At Some Point

At some point
comes the temptation
to stop
to cry and turn away
to yell "Uncle"
and see if the pain will stop
but living doesn't stop hurting
it just trades one ache for another
sharp stabs for dull throbs
being the grown-up is
accepting the pain one has
and keeping going
when what you really want
is to trade
the bruised days
and painful nights
for scraped knees
and baseball blisters.

Time Doesn't Run

Time doesn't run
or flow
or stand still
it is consumed
into some event horizon
that bends our universe
to its will
making us a faint glow
around a black, lightless center.

Working

Cubicles and partitions
divide the world
into paychecks
that keep schools fed
and stores open
while segmenting us
into windows
and non-windows
(far more common)
all for some purpose
we heard about once
that never seemed to apply
to what we actually do
or the rules we do it by
but those rules
make somebody else
so rich or powerful
we feel sorry for them
like Elvis or Clinton
whose fall consoles
those locked behind
flannel walls
and gray partitions.

052401

Driving my daughter to school
late already because of a lost CD
she has to have for dance class later
we see a rainbow
climbing into the dark day
bright enough to see the secondary
arching fainter alongside

and beyond the trees
the other end curving down
out of the black morning rain
lit by the rising sun behind us
two bright ends and a missing middle
sun behind, rain ahead, on we go
turning away to follow the road
a glimpse through the trees
and it is gone.

David Davis

I work for
the Program Evaluation Research Branch
in the Division of HIV/AIDS Prevention-Intervention, Research, and
     Support
of the National Center for HIV, STD, and TB Prevention
of the Centers for Disease Control and Prevention
an agency of the Department of Health and Human Services
of the United States Government
which means I work for
PERB/DHAP-IRS/NCHSTP/CDC/DHHS/USA
and am so far down the org chart
I'm not even on the PowerPoint presentation
and the branch website
is at least twelve clicks from the main page
if you know the shortcut
down where status is a real office
with walls that reach the ceiling
and a door that can be closed
and rank is obvious
just count the windows
and I have none.

Clearance

the trick is staying awake
box of an office
white noise generator
to kill the sounds of life
dances of decorum
that put courts in Europe
to shame
FreeCell, Minesweeper, and Solitaire
the only artificial stimulants
amid the Novocain
and laughing gas
of government gobbledygook
that lost all meaning
during the eighth rewrite
by the sixth bureaucrat
in the clearance process
making sure that no senator
or congressman of the realm
has any constituents
that could possibly be offended
by anything governmental
so we all look busy
and do the real work at home
or on weekends
subversively trying to save
a few lives
including our own
from official beige words
that say as little as possible
as laboriously as possible
about how to live and die
and stay awake

while working
for the government.

The CD

George Carlin isn't funny anymore
Mr. Conductor, the Hippy-Dippy Weatherman
now wants to waste people
to enjoy the chaos of mayhem
as if there were no mothers
who cry over dead fools
what has changed since our youth
have we watched too much TV news
seen too many horror movies
or is it backward
have we gotten harder
so more difficult to entertain
like Romans demanding thumbs down
is genocide acceptable public policy
for third-world nations
as the slow-motion Black Plague
tolls its bells
what happened when the first Black Death came
back around 534 AD
does so much death make death not matter
perhaps those grown so cold
should die
and decrease the surplus population.

Walking

The trouble with exercising at lunch
by walking around the parking lot
is that you stink the rest of the day
but if you don't exercise
you die
or get so stiff you look dead
either way, you begin to stink
so you stink either way
so I take my little walk
on even the hottest of days
and stink now
instead of later.

Toe Shoes

Satin-covered wood
padding and straps
pink slippers
to dream in
grace floating
in little girl nights
balanced on pain
and desire
because it is there
because it is hard
because somebody said
it is beautiful
pink clouds adrift
over hardwood earth
the young girls
go on toe.

Basketball

I keep trying to imagine my daughter
who at a prepubescent ten years old
is already five feet six tall
playing basketball
her back to the basket
using her weight to gain position down low
asking for the ball
so she can fake twice
drop her shoulder
spin around the shorter opponent
and finger roll
the ball into the net.
I guess that kind of thing
may be possible
heaven knows a little scholarship
would be nice
but somehow
I just can't see my little ballerina
pirouetting
for a fall-away jumper.

Inventory of Aches

Two ingrown toenails
One sore ankle
one stiff calf
multiple lower back pains
very stiff and sore right wrist
TMJ almost ready to quit
generally tired most of the time
in addition to the unfeeling
but worrying prostate enlargement
osteoporosis, and cholesterol
and the big one, the Stills
then there is Kathy's ADD
high cholesterol, diabetes
and depression
followed by Elizabeth's dyslexia
ADD, sleep problems, and stiff neck
my mother's bad back
history of falls
and turning eighty-three
and my sister
who is healthy as a horse
but borderline mentally retarded
and socially maladjusted
then, on the psychological side
there is the boring, dead-end job
I am stuck in
Kathy whining about wanting to retire
without explaining how
to keep Elizabeth in the special school
on just my government salary
and her retirement
when I could go on disability just any day

and the traffic to and from that school
plus the laundry, cooking, child care, trash taking out, car
            maintenance, house repair,
bill paying, shopping, and other chores that ended up in my lap
so Kathy would have time to do crafts and play Gameboy
that are keeping me from writing, or reading, or playing guitar
(as if my wrist could take that anymore)
on any of the other things that used to keep me sane
and semi-happy
with Elizabeth's sleep problems and Kathy's artificial hormone levels
I don't even get laid much anymore
so despite the two cars, three TVs, and paid-for house
I think I have earned
the right to be sad
which I would be
if my wrist and toes
would just stop hurting
long enough for me
to think about my
other aches.

The Girl

Dropping off my daughter at school
then driving to my office
I took the same route
same time
every day
and almost every day
I would see this girl
young woman actually
walking in the other direction
business suit, coat in winter
sneakers and backpack
probably walking to work
blond, short hair
lips naturally turned down
turning the lack of a smile
into a frown
good shape
(all that walking)
far too young for me
whoever she was
another human being
caught in a routine
not of her own making
treading the same sidewalks
day after day
difference is that she walked
while the rest of us drove by her
in our artificial, wheeled environments
with farther to go
or less time to give
then one day she was gone
never seen again
forever nameless

and unknown
new job?
new car?
Another blond mystery of life
never to be solved.

Simon Revised

It's a still-life watercolor
of a now-late afternoon
and the sun shines through the traffic haze
and pale dreams wash the room
and we sit and thirst for quiet
tasting lost years that have flown
leaving shells and little more
of the dangling days unfinished
the stranger inside the door
the echo of our lives
and you read your *Wall Street Journal*
and I my TV Guide
and we speak of household chores
in words worn bare and used
now the time is softly faded
I only see a shadow
I cannot feel my hand
in the dangling days unfinished
the stranger inside the door
the echo of our lives.

My Office

There is a picture of a girl
with her legs crossed
as a way to prevent AIDS
and other futile gestures
another of twelve kids
too young to know
where babies come from
saying they should know
how to prevent HIV
about a dozen pictures
of my daughter
a little more than one a year
baby to almost teen
measured in ballet costumes
notebooks of training courses
mostly unused and dusty
like most of what I can do
a thermometer
in a climate-controlled building
a calendar to measure my days
and a larger poster
promoting a play I wrote
back when I was alive
Not much of an office
which seems fitting
for the place and time.

On This Rock

Night rubs against the rough rock
like black acid
vapors rise unseen
scattering molecules
of what was
into the universe
to rejoin the ground of being
such is the rock nirvana
to be ground away
until there is no more there
there
the paradise
of not being
those who saw no reward
for those pebbles
that faded into dust
saw being there
as suffering
and those rocks
that have gone into the ground
tell no tales
of fiery underworlds
of volcanic rebirths
or cool streamsides
granite or limestone
they come and they go
like us
only slow.

At Fifty

At fifty years old
I wear out my wrist
playing computer games
between menial tasks
at my so-called occupation
while the books I want to read
stack up at home
the plays I want to write
sit blank on the page
and the thoughts I need to think
like the emotions I need to feel
are lost in the ether
of emails
and government time.

Dust and Ashes

When the human body
is subject to intense heat
say, exploding aviation fuel
followed by burning walls and floors
that get hot enough to melt steel
in very tall buildings,
about all that's left
is dust and ashes
that are scattered
to the streets below
and blown over the harbor.
This leaves, for some souls,
no body to be found
nothing to identify
nothing to bury,
leaving those awaiting

those who have blown away
tasting tears
amid the dust and ashes.
So to mourn
we don sackcloth
and ashes
we breathe the dust
of those who were
we taste bitter ashes
on our tongues
And take within ourselves
forever
the dust and ashes.

Shades of White

I paint with shades of white
lacking passion purple
from my box of colors
no envy green
or rage red
I range from light beige
to stark white
and a million shades
in between, all white.
So as I draw
on the black background
of this life
the visions get reversed
silhouettes of white on black
shadows brighter than their shade
negatives of what others see
the world switched
dark for light,
a limited, opposing view,
unexpected
but easy to read.

Anniversary, 2001

11/27/1986–11/23/2001
Fifteen years (about)
One and one half decades
new century
new millennium
Elizabeth eleven
going on sixteen
at least in size (five feet six?)
bigger than her babysitters

blooming, we hope
into a reading, writing, pre-teen
ready to throw us new problems
at the same time
we face the aged among us
those remaining
up in their eighties now
diminishing before us
becoming shades of our youth memory
preparing to vanish into dust
youth and age
and we stand between
a little past the middle
worn down, wearing out
holding on to a frayed rope
as the world unravels around us
from too many numbers
9/11, SF171, GS12, O6
like Elizabeth's nightmare
of a math test
stretching us like a rubber band
waiting for something to snap
us, them, or it
we try to patch things up
some scotch tape, a little patience
a dab of hot glue, a bit of love
keeping it together
doing what has to be done
waiting for the next big change
holding on to hope
and each other.

Midnight thirty

Mommy, if I can't get to sleep by midnight thirty,
can I come to your room?
asked the little girl
who was good at many things
but not at going to sleep
Yes, dear, but you have to wait
till you see midnight thirty
on your clock on the shelf.
It's nine thirty now, so you have plenty of time
to dream dreams and plan plans
to sing songs in your mind
and imagine being all grown up
and if you're still awake
at midnight thirty
then you may come to our room
and wake up Daddy
and he will get a blanket and pillow
and lie down on the floor
in your room
so you can sleep.
And so, content that there was salvation
if the dark went on too long
the little girl
peacefully
went to sleep.

The Office

In my office,
we are given doors
so we will not be distracted
from our work
by voices and people walking in the hall

but we are not allowed to close the doors
except when we are not in our office
for fear we will do something besides work.
In my office,
we have computers
connected to the Internet and email
so we can communicate with others
and find the information we need
to do our jobs
but our key-strokes are recorded
and emails public records
so that we don't do anything
unofficial electronically.
In my office
we have to check our mailboxes
at least twice a day
for notices and forms
that need processing
but we have to be sure
the mail room is kept dark
and the door closed
to save someone else's energy.
And in my office
we are supposed to be
happy, motivated professionals
with little chance of a raise
and retirement the great reward.
And in my office
the administration
is always puzzled
when we keep looking
for other jobs.

My Job

I work in PERB/DHAP-IRS/NCHSTP/CDC/HHS
as a GS-12
providing TA and TT for CBA to CBOs and HDs
who get funding from CDC for HIV/AIDS prevention
under PAs 01001 and above
I also work with the OC in the DHAP OD
on evaluating health comm.
But mainly, as a health comm. spec.
my job
is to make things clear.

Random Thoughts upon Entering 2002

Palindromes will abound in 2002, more than in 1991. If I have survived one palindromic year, I guess I can stand another.

Being rich means more than having the money to buy what you want, it means having space in which to put all the stuff you buy.

The most dangerous thing I do is drive in Atlanta traffic. Terrorists from Arabia don't scare me near as much as secretaries talking a mile a minute on cell phones while driving 85 on I-85.

Things will start to change more this year. I will get a raise, Elizabeth will turn twelve and we will no longer have a little girl but a young woman for a daughter, and my mother and Kathy's aunt will become very old. We stand on the doorstep of a still-dark house, looking for the light switch.

On the second day of 2002, Elizabeth and I went walking in the snow. It was evening, just before sunset, the snow still falling, the ground already white. We walked down the street to the little swim and tennis club so we could watch the snow falling on the little creek that runs nearby. It was barely cold enough for snow, so not yet the burning cold that would come after dark. She caught snowflakes on her tongue and we both ate a hand-full of snow from a railing. We talked about how snow was magic, covering the brown on normal life with glowing white, making the world not only different, but pretty, hiding the mud and grime underneath. Southern snow is especially wonderful because it melts before it can get dirty, unlike the snow up North that stays around all winter and becomes gray and polluted. In the South, snow is always white and beautiful and fun, while it's there. Then it is gone, leaving only a memory of what was, a retouched photograph of a magic moment of memory.

The next day the neighbors were out with a little plastic sled for their daughter to play on. In exchange for use of our steeper driveway, they let Elizabeth take turns with Chelsy riding the snow on the blue, molded plastic. Such delight all around. Sliding on snow, rolling in snow, getting snow all over, working that rare commodity for all the joy it could hold. Snowman; made one. Snow angel, made one of those too. Snow to eat, snow to throw, five glorious inches of snow to gladden the heart of every child who ever had a snow day. Such brief happiness, not forty-eight hours of snow, precious because it was so brief. Let us praise snowmen and snowballs and children who wish for white Christmases and gods of winter who deliver only a few days late, and let us hope the rest of the year goes as it began, in surprise, delight, wonder, beauty, and the excitement of the child.

The Day After

The day after getting a raise,
I find myself writing the blues
well, money won't buy . . . you know
what depresses me is the waste
of my time
of which I feel little left
At the office
I cannot read plays
or novels or history
or science or poetry
or newspapers or magazines
only memos, emails, and abstracts
At the office
I am not supposed to write
poetry or plays
in prose or pentameter
only peer-reviewed articles
and statements of work
for contractors to follow
I am to attend meetings
which are actually OK
in that they keep me awake
In the office
my door must stay open
so I cannot nap or sing or scratch
where it itches
or any of those other human things
we do when we control our lives
no, Uncle Sam owns me
eight and a half hours a day
(thirty minutes for lunch)
he pays sort of OK
though we all believe we could do better

on the outside
if they had jobs like this
on the outside
So we accumulate annual leave
and count years, then months, then days
until retirement
praying to god
there is still something of us left
on that glorious day.

Entropy and Atrophy

Sitting here listening to my brain turn to mush, so desperate I consider a game of solitaire a form of mental stimulation, even as it wears out my hand from clicking the mouse over and over, I ponder how we are universes in miniature, slowly dissolving into chaos as entropy wins its eternal battle with order. As skills decay from lack of use, like muscles tied to a bed, so time, age, and a government job siphon off what strength there was. Energy fades the struggle to preserve order slowly lost in emails and obscurity. I used to have long hair, play guitar, study physics, read science fiction, act in plays, and write poetry and drama. I taught in universities. I chased women. I had dreams, plans, promise. Now I am bald, have arthritic fingers, study *Discover Magazine*, barely read the newspaper, am too unhealthy to act, and write these little snippets in those moments my job comes to a crashing hurry-up-and-wait. I earn my living as a "Health Communications Specialist," a job nobody knows what is, including me. I am lucky if I have the energy to chase my wife when the kid isn't looking. My life is becoming a slow descent into disorder at the same time that I am feeling my wits and abilities draining away like water from a leaky faucet. My typing is slowing and more and more dependent on the spell-checker. I make stupid mistakes. I am getting clumsy. I am no longer a safe driver. I want to get away and have nowhere to go but home and then back to work the next day. I live from vacation to vacation and dedicate those to showing my daughter the world. This too shall pass; she will grow up and leave home. But by then there will be little left of me, just a shell of what used to be, an ill old man with no dreams, no plans, no promise.

Before My Eyes

Before my eyes
during the space
of some Nickelodeon music video
by some barely pubescent boy group
artificially manufactured by some producer
she changes
the metamorphosis begins
my hand on her shoulder
she suddenly giggles
"He's so cute," she says
of some Hollywood clone
selected by focus groups
and mall intercepts
as being the cute one
he may even sing on key
though the sound is so layered
and reengineered
it's impossible to tell
what his real voice would be like
but he's cute
I give him that
cute enough to move my daughter
from boy-hating
to adolescent crush
"He's probably a jerk," she continues,
"but he's sooooo cute."
An image of her teen years
flashes before me
boys and jerks
and how to tell
one from another
an essential skill
that must be learned

with at least a dash
of bitter experience
she giggles again
and blushes at her own
budding femininity
she will be OK, I think
so wise already
to know jerkdom
is possible
even in the terminally cute
she will grow painfully
wiser yet
but she will be OK
but my own pain
changes
with a shift
almost as profound
the little girl
daddy's little girl
is leaving
and the teen
is inward bound.

High Holidays

Chinese New Year
Ash Wednesday
Valentine's Day
Three high holidays
and no days off
Friday off to Boston
The Cape in winter
(Did Homer paint that?
Everybody else did.
At least those hardy enough
to be there
to see the flakes
on the foam.)
New England painters
have a landscape
in miniature
grays and greens
and think it grand
One western sunset
over the Superstitions
would break their pallet
but we are off to Boston
then a bus to Plymouth
pilgrims no longer
but regular guests
come to see the relatives
or what is left of them
one dear, frail woman
hanging on
within sight of the bay
where half a rock
lies encased in glass
to honor men and women

who managed to hang on
(even though they were not first
as any Virginian can tell you
and frequently does.)
So we brave February
when no tourists come
and half the town is closed
to help the aunt
last of her family
descendent of Coast Guard Engineers
and French-Canadians
who spent her days
finding mothers for orphans
and is now orphan herself
not quite alone
but barely standing
by the rocky coast
looking at a short future
and a long past
needing the kind of help
you only ask relatives for
So AirTran provides
and off we go
cold winds blow
in more ways
than one.

In Plymouth

In Plymouth
the rain was cold
by night it would be snow
and the puddles ice
in the morning
we played in the indoor pool
too small to swim in
flips, handstands, floating
was all you could do
between the visits
to my wife's aunt
now bent and twisted
by age and scoliosis
we bought her shoes
wheat-free noodles
and a few hours
outside the old folks home
eating steak and lobster
instead of hot dogs and beans
then flew home
through oceans of security
that left us feeling insecure
and sore footed
from long lines
and shoe inspections
it was warm, sort of,
at home
but it rained the next day
a reminder
that drops fall everywhere
and a brochure came
in the mail
promoting long-term care insurance

another reminder
of what comes everywhere
the drops that fill
the fertile flood plains
bending our heads
twisting us
in the current.

Stages

My wife gave me a list
of the stages of adolescence
purporting to describe
the psychological changes
the normal teenager
goes through
on the path to maturity
having missed most of these stages myself
I found it very instructive
the slow process
to independence
sexuality
and responsibility
that is necessary
for the girl
to become the woman
and the child
to become the adult
and the father
to become
the sad old man.

The Job

What I hate about this job
is that it demands
I spend my time
for most of each day
somewhere besides
the places where
I could be doing
something worth
my time.

Winter Olympics

The skeleton is a sled
ridden by people
who need sheer terror
on a daily basis
but one such woman
of Olympic quality
wrote my daughter
an email
to help her with a report
on the skeleton
for school
during the Winter Games
in 2002
and made my daughter
happy and proud
and wanting to watch
her new friend
the skeleton rider
who deserves a Gold medal
for small blessings
and kind words

as well as the Silver
she received
for flying
fast and low.

The Promotion

By dent of hard work, supreme effort,
and hanging around long enough
to pick up the tricks
I have been promoted
to an office
with a window.
This, in my little corner
of the government
is status
to see the sky
reflected in the windows
of the building
across the way
to crane my neck
and be able to see clouds
to know rain is falling
before I go outside
this is recognition
that I have arrived
I have topped out
in the climb
up the government ladder
so that for the next fourteen years
as I collect my step increases
on the road to retirement
I will at least be able
to see the world outside
pass me by.

The Period

On May 2, 2002,
in the middle of dance class
my daughter got
her first period
it did not make her happy
though she knew what it was
and had been half expecting it
and knew to roll up some toilet paper
and stick it in her panties
until I came to pick her up
At eleven years old
she is young for this
ahead of the already tightening curve
she enters puberty
almost before adolescence
Now she is worried
about going swimming tomorrow
about carrying pads in her backpack
about leaving for Costa Rica
with her classmates next week
this growing up stuff is messy
not fun at all
marking calendars
counting days
who knew in third grade
this is what adding double digits
was good for
but she is now in fifth grade
suddenly not sure
turning twelve is a good idea
but no more able to slow time
than her parents
who try to deal

with such milestones
as how to get blood
out of panties
calmly, unembarrassed
knowing we get one shot at this
each step a unique event
never to be repeated
while we face a triple-vision
the slightly worried daughter of today
facing some new part of life
our memory of the little girl of yesterday
who had no concerns
beyond where her blanket went to
and our image of a future woman of tomorrow
shyly counting the days
her period is late.

Bleeding Time

Bleeding time
sutured to an ergonomic chair
preventing HIV with thumb twiddles
as poems, plays, health, and life
slide under the doorway
into the four strong winds
leaving remnants
of what will never be
moments of caresses
lie untouched on the plate
like asparagus
words unspoken, untyped
fade like the canals on Mars
in the glare of empty time
our lives are what is left
when what was not
is scraped away
potential does not become kinetic
energy is converted to entropy
and slides into the quantum void
unconserved, lost
like these hours
listening to the mouse click
a life lit by cathode rays
earning my tucker
by sitting silent
and not doing
what needs to be done.

For L. C.

Listening to Leonard Cohen
leering in his voice
as it gravels out words
that rip veneer
and cut like ice
showing us a dark mirror
twisted so the image
bends back on itself
to show our other side
the side behind the side
sentences polished
into black pearls
that awe us
with their rarity
of shape
though somehow
the necklace that holds them
keeps breaking
letting them roll away
jewels on their own
dancing to a monotone tune.

Fireflies

Green velvet dark
mating lights waltzing
love's fireworks
on shirtless nights

turn out the lights
if we can't see the stars
maybe this will do
Tinkerbell in the woods

and we are lost boys
chasing fairy dust
that sparkles
among the leaves

minuscule lightning
but no jar tonight
precious glory flies free
lighting memory

Daughter, can you ever know
how precious miracles are
lovelights of home
flit on the darkening sky.

Catastrophes

Catastrophes happen in slow motion too
Not just the tornado blur or hurricane whip
Not the bullet crack or fender crunch
Not the movie slo-mo of fast frames replayed slowly
but the creeping time of diabetes
eroding feet like the gentle stream

wears away the solid land above
like cholesterol erects its dams
of twigs too small for beaver bites
forming fault lines in the heart
But there is no FEMA
for these disasters taking years
no emergency shelter
no soup kitchen
for those who trickle away
on calm days
in the sunshine.

Pictures

All around my office
are pictures
of Elizabeth
one or two
for every year
a school picture
a dance class picture
family shots
from babe
to "babe"
ballerina
to basketball
one girl
at every age
constant change
constant yet
the same
in every age.

Dyslexia

When the kaleidoscope spins
throwing light around like balls
in a kid's fun factory
it's hard to see the star
in the dark beyond the light
to see the future lit by the past
a far-off blaze that will only show up
after the evening sun has set
and we turn our eyes to the night
but sometimes
beyond the prisms and mirrors
there is a hint of what will come
further along
"Elizabeth reads well," the teacher said
and the galactic glow pierced the day
promising starlight
hinting at a star
beyond the light of day.

Standardized

When we measure life in stanines
and growth in grade levels
on standardized tests
what have we learned
We have learned that sometimes
patience and persistence pay off
we have learned that
learning by whatever measure
can occur despite whatever
we have learned that
sheer guts comes in all forms
we have learned that
we have not measured life
but some part of living
and that pride in those we love
can have no measure.

When I Consider

When I consider how my time is spent
in vacant days and empty nights
like some computer geek
addicted to electronic solitaire
projecting an illusion of purpose
manipulating some system
as if reason existed
for colored screens
and multiple clicks
an artificial image
computer generated
a special effect
applied to an imaginary life.

Anniversary Poem 2002

These are the times that try men's souls
the winter of our discontent
when the sunshine spouses
and summer lovers
shiver in the cold of change
jobs change, schools change
houses change, health changes
life changes and age changes us
we are sandwiched
between elderly women
and a budding girl
caught up in wars and revolutions
overwhelmed by isolation
in the crowd and traffic
time, time, time, see what's become of us
running low on possibilities
we are not what we were
and never will be what we thought
creeping past middle-age
living on pills to raise or lower
the level of this or that
letting go of dreams one by one
no longer doing what we want
or what we can
or even what we need to
only what has to be
and barely that
no time left to feel or care
too cold to touch
just get through the day
make it to the weekend
then to Christmas
then to April

just get by, somehow
without cracking up
not really living
watching moments
that should be memories
slip slide away
lost forever
to lives with hints of ends
in this our Valley Forge
the virtue is in hanging in
making it through
soldiering through the winter
marching shoulder to shoulder
toughing it out
tentmates in the frozen dark
hoping to someday
cross the Delaware
march to Yorktown
retire to some Mount Vernon
on a hill
overlooking a river
having the wisdom
to walk away
together.

Christmas

Stories inside stories, myths within myths
babes in mangers, old bishops, coins in shoes
presents under trees, jolly old men from cartoons
and Coke ads, poems claimed by judges
who never wrote the like
What the old scriptures said had to be
so the new scriptures must be true
those who wrote them believed
so stories are based on stories
that, like Troy and locust eaters
may have some basis in fact, or not
but myths are myths
not because they are factual or false
but because they tell something true
about the teller of the stories
so we repeat the songs of angels
tell the tales of shepherds
build legends around barber poles
in the far north where only submarines go
in order to say something
about ourselves
We do not lie in these tall tales
but speak a truth that goes beyond the facts
like Eden and the apple
it does not matter so much
if the snake is real
but what it said
so Bethlehem may be historical
or another movie-Santa's workshop
what matters is
that we believe
some deity from the great beyond
reached down and touched the earth

and made us precious
and that is the truth
we tell about ourselves
on Christmas morns.

Calling Schools

Calling schools to ask
who wants to teach
my daughter
for the next six years
reveals a problem
they seem to think
I should be grateful
they would even consider
admitting her
and I am convinced
they are the ones
receiving the privilege.

Dry Tears

Dry tears, evening
Bowed, bent, broken
Walking sunset
Holding two hands
Breaking trail
For one

Go on.

Roswell Reels (2003–2022)

The Problem

The problem is
that I still see
with eyes that
remember running
down the sidewalk
free and easy
only once
that remember the prom
and improvising poetry
about her face
in the Sambo's
at midnight afterward
on our only date
that remember the snow
outside the hospital window
they opened
during the alcohol bath
to lower my fever
that remember the sunrise
over New Mexico
driving alone
across the country
searching for a job
these are the eyes that see
not some old man's eyes
they see a past
that has not aged
and does not like
today's visions
that still search
for possibilities
not the inevitable.

Glancing Out the Window

Glancing out the window at the shapely smoker on the steps below I
    wonder
if smoker's nipples taste different
like the stale, deflating breath that issues from their lips
does the nicotine and tar pervade their body
tainting the other body parts commonly licked or sucked
during various activities I never engaged in
with women addicted to the weed
this strikes me as an odd thought at first
then upon reconsideration I decide
that contemplating the flavor of breasts
is a typical masculine diversion
indulged in when there is no opportunity
to test the hypothesis
since I know nothing about this female
except her shape outlined across the courtyard
and her devotion to a drug-induced habit
that makes her unattractive to my eyes
despite the curve, or savor, of her tits.

House Hunting

Ah! The thrill of the hunt
through other people's attics
seeking in closets and cabinets
the elusive hardwood
the desirable jacuzzi
counting bedrooms and bath
balancing three-quarter acre lots
against level driveways
fenced yards and finished basements
lots of storage but few stairs
master on main, den and deck
could we put bookshelves
where cabinets now reside
gas or electric, one oven or two
while around us stare the images
of lives lived
paraphernalia of what was
the kids and grandkids
toys and trophies
that would have to go
to make way for our
nics and nacs
graven memories
of the semantic shift
from house to home.

Sailing Away

Sailing away over the asphalt
riding the wild Greyhound
to the unknown South
She set out for adventure
suitcase and sleeping bag

stowed away below
mates seated around
guide and helmsman to the fore
off for adventure
equipped with stamps and phone cards
trail mix and labeled underwear
ready for the wilds of Americus and St. Simon
Brunswick and the coast
to see past and present
nature and history
the one week mini-continental tour
of selected sites within easy driving range
of the familiar elementary school
the great graduation expedition
before settling down
to the responsibilities of middle school
ready for one last adventure
before childhood's end
and full price at buffet bars
one giant step toward independence
and adolescence
and all the obligations thereof
to rebel and talk on the phone
so with a little tear
off she goes to adventure
leaving hearth and home
parents and TV
for the wilds of South Georgia
and the one-week trip
that is only one step
on the long journey
to adventure.

Dark Clouds

Dark clouds
wind
remnants of tornados
that killed in Kansas City
now blowing over Atlanta
scaring the birds and wives
bragging of destruction
houses splintered
cars transported
mobile homes never to be found
and bodies lying quietly
under bathtubs
bare of walls
waiting to be found.

I Try Verse

When the dialogue won't come
I try verse
writing out the junk
getting past the obvious
putting the first ideas down
to get to the new
writing with fingers
not thoughts
reestablishing the process
of connecting A to Upsilon
via Connecticut using pi glue
on a cold Monday in May
somewhere south of the Arctic
waiting for the bell
not to ring.

I Shake

I shake inside
like a Parkinson's hand
nerves gone
synapses exhausted
out of ammo
wobbling like the last
person in the Ironman
running only to finish
to complete the course
I have not won
the spectators have gone home
the TV crews driving off
I hope there are still two women
waiting at some finish line
I can no longer imagine
but it is dark now
and there are no stars.

New and Old

New and old don't mix
Fixing up the old house to sell
while trying to unpack into the new
leaves both incomplete
like my daughter
searching for new classes
      new lockers
      new friends
at a new school
but talking to the old friends
on the phone each night
Sometimes the small moves
are the hard ones
without the clean breaks
      or new beginnings
The old drags at us
      like baggage
that should have been left behind
      but wasn't
because we were only
      moving twenty miles.

In Less than a Month

In less than a month
she will be thirteen
officially a teen
neigh six feet tall
bigger and stronger
than her old man
still not sure about seventh grade
middle school, middle youth
moving into volleyball and basketball

holding on still to dance
transitions and changes
holding on and letting go
no more children's prices
now she eats and sleeps grownup
PG-13 the movies say
and I try to remember
that it is the PG
that still counts.

Kathy

Kathy's riding the yo-yo again
string taunt, lots of spinning
whirling in place inches off the floor
then flying up to spin around the world
looping the loop around us
a dazzling display of motion
stable only while rotating
searching for control
by going faster and faster
terrified
of being silent and still.

Mars

I have been looking for Mars
which is very close I am told
but every day the storms roll in
confounding any vision of heaven
throwing down lightning and rain
violent flashes, threats of flood
little explosions in the sky
that block the sight
of oncoming Mars.

Addresses

Corona Street, Kim Court
School Drive, Hunter's Ridge
Stadium Drive
other addresses long forgotten
(Was it Main St. in Carolina Beach?
I was five and probably never knew)
Cedar Creek we lived next to the graveyard
which was between the pastor's house and the church
Portsmouth was on the Academy campus
converted barracks, live-in faculty
with sixteen-year-old cadets all around
At Chesapeake was on the College grounds
in a warehouse converted to a duplex
with a railroad track out front
School Drive was exactly that
the drive into the junior high
I walked across to attend
Corona was just a street in a development
a little loop of stucco houses
we had the hole of an unfinished pool
in the backyard
Stadium Drive was at college
a dorm room for five years
for me a stable address
Grad school was behind a church
where I sang in the choir
the forgotten address a basement
one small room with a bath and kitchen
big enough to turn around in
no stove, just a hotplate and fridge
Then two years in an apartment in Mauldin
too close to the school where I taught
never live in the district where you teach

good advice, but somehow sad
Then another forgotten address in Carbondale
upstairs in an apartment complex
The complex next door had a pool
we did not, but it was quiet
once the wife-beater moved out
Livingston was another second-floor
one bedroom, laundry downstairs
where I met my wife, who was pretty
though a little broad abeam
I thought as she walked away
hiding her clean panties in the basket
Then the year in Tuscaloosa
with Kathy and a cat, new experiences
Off to Union College, upstairs again
but now four rooms, good size
one an office, one a living room for guests
who never came.
Union didn't work, so, to Greenwood
in the "mixed" complex, not the "white" one
but in the town, not in the cotton fields
or campus where the black faculty lived
in town with the whites
Finally, giving up on something
to Atlanta and Kathy, cram into her place again
six months this time
Find a house, Kim Court, four bedrooms
split level, wooded hillside, low maintenance
lots of space till Elizabeth arrived
Was it fifteen years there? A record for me
A good house, but not for children
especially not for playing outside
Finally to Hunters Ridge Court
longest name of all, biggest house
close, relatively, to the new school

private, handles learning disabilities
what we needed, but off in Roswell

Lots of houses, apartments, dorms
too many for one life
settled now, soon, for now
for now we enter a new phase
suburban father, housewife, teen
hoping the house will fit.

Traffic

Red and white rivers
crosscurrents flowing
in the dark evening
never touching, we hope
no churning into metal eddies
no waves crashing over us
just swift streams
lighting the way home.

Two Signs Dylan Was Right

Arby's, Sunday afternoon
two couples, adjacent booths
black and white
and white and black

Another restaurant
a big white guy
and a big black guy
holding hands across the table
while saying grace
over the Chinese food.

Mid-Life

I think that I shall have
a mid-life crisis
and become
a dirty old man
who stares at women's breasts
looking down their shirts
and commenting politely
on their attractive shapes
Perhaps I shall go to strip clubs
and place dollar bills
under the garters
of those who wear nothing else
or buy those videos
of girls gone wild
enough to flash any camera
that offers a free T-shirt
Perhaps even visit an XXX store
to rent videos of people having sex
I hear the ones from Eastern Europe
are so fresh the performers
are still enjoying themselves
In my dreams I shall chase
and even catch beautiful women
who do not remember twenty years of me
to whom I am new and exciting
a "mature" man who appreciates women
who knows they are so much more
than bodies or parts
but loves the parts and bodies
anyway.

17 (Anniversary 2003)

Is prime
Indivisible
A unit
As is three
as in you, me, and E
(or five, if you count the cats)
so we are a prime family in a prime year
the year when everything changed
you retired to a life of hard housewife labor
we moved to new house in new town near new school
new, changed, different, adjust, adapt, unpack
Elizabeth learning to hit the books harder
between basketball, volleyball, and dance
trying to find where her large frame fits
in the middle school social whirl
You unpacking and repacking your life, box by box
seeking the magic that transforms house to home
seeking sounds to break the silence of an empty house
seeking your own niche in the Saddle Creek social whirl
and now my mother, moving next year, more change
more packing and unpacking, more stuff to put away or use
more sofas and mirrors to shift around
It's supposed to get better soon, isn't it?
One, soon two, houses to sell
after a last Christmas in Greer
Yes, it is supposed to get better soon
but on cool nights
when I snuggle next to you for warmth
and fall asleep with my arm around you
I know I can live with this
After all, fifty-three is a prime age
2003 is a prime year
so we must be entering our prime time.

Beach

On the white sand
crowded with bikinis
and an occasional thong
she sat back from the waves
on a large towel
shaded by a big umbrella
covered with a Moslem scarf
high-neck shirt
and long pants
modesty intact
among the bare infidels
as she breastfed
her new baby.

Writing Out the Junk

Writing out the junk
Digging for bedrock
By tossing out the first
Then second
Then third idea
Going for oil
Or diamonds
Down deep
Where the rocks are hot
And the pressure steep
Where the digging takes drills
And men sweat
And die.

Anniversary 2004

We have become so traditional
you and I
in this our eighteenth year
ranch house in the suburbs
commute to the office for me
take care of the house and kid for you
basketball and shopping at the mall
sewing and quilting
TV in the bedroom
low hormones, diabetes, and prostate problems
like we were getting old or something
At least we haven't started voting Republican, yet.
But we have settled into aging
parenting a teen
dealing with retirement
Soon we will be the old ones
as, sadly, those who came before
leave one by one, each in their own time.
We are embers glowing,
warming each other in the night
past our hot blaze,
not yet eyeing the red of sunset
but seeing the shadows lengthen now
feeling the chill of fall,
arm in arm, planning for ends, not beginnings,
except for the other, the child, now youth,
waiting for the greenwood to catch
for the flame to be passed
and keep our light burning
savoring each day before the fledgling flies.
We are not yet old, but no longer young
We are parents, but no longer of a child
We have been together so long
we can no longer be alone.

The Way It Is

Somewhere I just got tired
Maybe it was those nights rocking the kid who didn't go to sleep
Or reading *Harry Potter* to her night after night till my voice gave way
But more likely it was the Still disease flares
Either the first, or, more likely, the second
I don't think I ever recovered from that second one
I never quite lost the weight again
Or got the muscles back
Just the aches
The knees hurt going up stairs now
And I have to wear an undershirt even in the summer
To stay warm in the air conditioning
And six in the morning comes too early
And I just got tired and never recovered
And that is just the way it is.

My Image

My image in the mirror looks sad
like some old man worn out by time
the shoulders droop, the back curves
a fun-house image gone bad
the trouble is, I feel worse than I look
an arthritic on a bad day before a storm
too sore to sit, too tired to stand
dozing off if I even blink
there's tired, and then there's tired
and I'm tired
they say Chekov, at the end
would take all day to write three lines
alas, I am not Chekov
I scribble only words of no note
and mourn how brilliantly I fail.

Watching My Daughter

Watching my daughter play basketball
it occurs to me
how much difference
confidence makes
she seems to have
my fatal flaw
of thinking too much
about what she does not know
the hesitation
to evaluate all the possibilities
to look for the safe choice
staying within the confines
of her coaching
and never
just driving to the basket.

In the End

In the end
it is not life or time or wisdom
that is lost
it is memories
no one else will ever know
that disappear
crying alone on the street corner
the spring break I first kissed a nipple
listening to my father haggle over bongos in Mexico
taking supper to my father when he worked in the jail
seeing my mother literally kneeling in prayer one early morning
rocking my daughter to sleep singing a Paul Simon song
gone are the days
and no one else will know
to mourn their passing.

I Remember Running

I remember running
it was down a sidewalk
across from a school
toward a friend's house
a sunny spring afternoon
not far from home
past green bushes and lawns
in front of the little houses
of fifty years ago about
fourth grade maybe
feeling wind, moving freely
legs and arms gliding
a sprint of maybe fifty yards
just a boy running
as boys do
and the reason I remember
is I had been sick the winter before
tired, sore, fevered
and this was the first time
I had run in months
and as far as I remember now
the last.

Spring is Back

Spring is back
the A/C is humming
fat women wear short sleeves
storm alerts squall at evening
pollen blooms
ah yes, spring.

The Rain Is Creeping In

The rain is creeping in
cloud shadows sweep across the ground
my daughter once asked
Daddy, did you ever chase a cloud?
No, I said, but I did used to watch
    the cloud shadows fly across the brown mountains
    in the deserts of Arizona
even wrote a long-forgotten poem about it
    though I did not tell her that part
But chase a cloud? Don't they go too fast
    or fade away and reform
    or merge so you can't tell one from another?
To run after an edge of light
    passing through a moment of life
    lost way up in the sky
How childish
Like writing a poem
or dreaming in the day.

I Have Gone Back

I have gone back to writing
    with a pen
Ink on paper, the old-fashioned way
    one-handed thought
To see if it makes any difference
    in what comes out
No bits or bytes, keys or mice
    of the modern media
Lined paper, ink encased in plastic
    and hard thought
The message in the old medium
    Kilroy and I were here.

At Rise

At rise we see
At rise we see
or maybe we don't
maybe we feel
or taste
our gut twisting
as the curtain rises
bile filling our mouths
creating a scene
a tragedy of the senses
a comedy of odors
assaulting us
bitter words
foul language
sandpaper on skin
catharsis of whatever
running down our leg
or not
maybe we just see.

For Tyke (Katherine Elizabeth Bixby, 1919-2005)

The daylilies and roses were blooming
along the driveway
as we packed up your things
in the little apartment
where you died
Kathy knew the story of each item
as it was wrapped and boxed
to send to Atlanta
and our basement
A couple of days after the funeral
we went whale watching
off Provincetown
finback, humpback
and a glimpse of a minke
a very good day, they said
Some people watching on shore of course
tattoos and tatters
couples holding hands
      men and women
        women and women
      men and men
        women and men
Traditional Provincetown
steamers and gelato
T-shirts and kites
(I bought two heavy coats on a hot day in July)
Sunday we went to Chatham
no whales, boring people
but one shop that sold T-shirts
with rubbings of fish
then to see Paul Bailey
(Father Paul, the priest)
your old friend

who did the funeral
with five other priests
(you were well remembered
even the assisted living home staff cried
we had to give them a box of Kleenex)
Your old, old friends were there
from Catholic Charities
from the beach at Sagamore
even from Immanuel
Everyone said what a good person you were
but they all cited different reasons
On Monday the moving van came
and took away what was now ours
(David took his share the day after the funeral
he was actually well-behaved
satisfied with the lawyer
and nice to Kathy
she was so relieved)
Now you lie on the hill in Hyde Park
with Ahgie, your mother, your father
and your grandmother
sharing the same headstone
Kathy was with you when you died
that early Monday morning
Paul did well with the funeral
David and Kathy divided your lot peacefully
Everything is taken care of
You lived and died wisely and well
Rest now
We will remember.

Ides of September

On the Ides of September
I contemplate days and years
As my daughter nears a birthday
Marking fifteen years of breathing
And I stare at half a century
Plus half a decade of being
(How many days is that? How many memories that I have already forgotten? What portion of my life is past? How much longer will I have with my wife, with my daughter? Will I die first? Will I be there for graduations, for a wedding, a birth?)
Trite and trivial thoughts
Compared to the sunrises and sunsets
The earth has seen
Or the billions of memories lost forever
Unrecorded, untold, unknown
Of all who have come and gone
Since some sunrise over an African plain
Seen by some naked Eve as she picked up an obsidian scraper
By a morning fire
As the stars faded in the dawn
And she wondered
Where her life was going
She had no way of imagining
Pyramids, longboats, letterpresses, suspension bridges, libraries, skyscrapers, Internets
Or even what the stars really are
Nor can I see thousands hence years or millions
What will we be when stars flicker out
We calculate from Big Bangs to icy entropy
But see not past the sunset
Tomorrow is the eternal mystery
Constant surprise
Leaving me a speck in time

A single moment called now
To kiss the girls good morning
And pray I make it home
To kiss the girls good night.

A Line

A line, sea and sky
water salty as blood
beating against land
I kneel on cracked shells
that once held something
grains of worn-out rocks
slip-slide through toes
the wind blows past
evaporating drops of me.

Images of Memory

Walking home in Tucson
past the bookstore that put out free books
covers torn off, in a box on the sidewalk
sandals flapping the three or four blocks
to the church, my apartment a block behind
one flight underground, hot plate, mini fridge
bed, desk, dresser, trunk, wardrobe, BW TV
one chair for the desk, no table or tub
black widows on the stairs, and one day
snow on the palms, and me in sandals.

ANNIVERSARY 2005

Nineteen years
What an odd number
But also prime
One short of a big round number
Not quite a double decade
Not quite a milestone
But worth noting nonetheless
For its own odd qualities

Suddenly we sit in cafes talking basketball
    Like we actually knew something about it
Sadly we have no reason to go to Cape Cod
    Except it's sort of pretty in the summer
Slowly we are getting grayer, stiffer, sorer
    Some illness the doctors call age

Our time is now scheduled by high school coaches
Our health comes from pills prescribed by a dozen physicians
Our freshman jock spouts Latin and literature
Our futures hold more endings than beginnings

So, as we mark another day after Thanksgiving
In the pause between turkey and basketball
After taking Elizabeth to practice and Mom and Donna home
If we ever get a quiet moment alone
Let us remember that we have survived many rocks on the road
Hung together despite everything
And even worn out a mattress in the process

Here's to odd prime numbers
And hopes to see a few more
Amongst the big round ones.

Passage—First Driving Lesson

On the Fourth of July
expressing his independence
the basketball player
we watched in the boys' varsity games
after the girls played
choosing to be free of restraint
died unbuckled

On Saturday the eighth
in an empty lot
behind a medical building
across from the hospital
I handed my fifteen-year-old
clutching her still-warm permit
the keys to the car
for the first time
as soon as she was strapped in
praying to the god of seatbelts
airbags, and adolescents
and spent the first lesson
teaching how to brake.

Twenty Years (Anniversary 2006)

Twenty years
Two decades
A generation
Five-fourteenths of my life
Twenty-fifty-thirds of yours
Five-fourths of Elizabeth's
A long time
One of those round-number milestones
Where one celebrates
Not the original event
but the endurance
the durability
the adaptability
the persistence
the determination
the commitment.

We did not start out to end up here
half-retired suburban basketball groupies
chauffeuring a teen through adolescence
connoisseurs of buffet restaurants
looking for shortcuts around traffic jams
me hanging on at CDC with arthritic fingers
you the Team Mom fighting diabetes
Elizabeth the great kid with dyslexia
We did not start out to end up here
We started out to
      take the trip together
      keep each other warm at night
      deal with whatever came
      try to understand
      and to love each other

And we have.

Blossoms

Crabapple blossoms
Coat the lawn like snowflakes
White drifts piled on steps.

To Elizabeth

You put words in our hearts
Dreams in our hands
We were childhood and youth
Lived again
Thanks and love
    Are not enough
But you have
    What we can give.

Mom and Dad
09/2008
For Yearbook

An Old Picture

It's an old picture, black and white
1920-something, bright sunny day
my mother the girl
three sisters and little brother
(where were the three older sisters?)
smiling at having their picture taken
an event back then
especially for mountain kids
so poor they wouldn't notice
when the Depression came
Here they are, still young
elementary school age it looks
happy, grinning, outside in play clothes
eyes alight in sunshine, summer
not seeing past that day
no shadows in this photograph
no image of the car crash
that will kill the youngest girl
bright eyes looking directly at the camera
or the mysterious tropical disease
that will carry away the only son
while in the army just after WWII
despite the Tom Sawyer smile and overalls
Even those who shine in my memory
have eyes not yet darkened
by cancer or war or ill children or dead husbands
My mother lives on
She will be eighty-nine this summer
changed so that this girl
in the picture
needs a name on the back
to be recognized
but it is her

eighty or so years ago
bright and sunny
the way I never knew her
her sun still on the rise.

2007

Twenty-one years
thrice lucky seven
but the past today seems past
we live today, but see tomorrow
we live today
    the quilter, Team Mom, and teen chauffeur
    the writer, CDC employee, and algebra helper
    the high school junior, honor student, and basketball center
but we see
    driver's licenses, voter registration, college applications
Change is coming
    but not yet.
    visible as a mast tip
    over the horizon
the nest is not empty
    but the unfledged bird
    is flapping her wings

So, we savor the now
    each moment we are still three
    each math problem needing help
each basketball game needing taping
each Shakespeare play, car ride when she talks, dinner out, family vacation
Change is coming
    but not yet

We two became one became three
Lovers to spouses to parents of baby, child, girl, teen, almost legal adult
Change is coming
    but not yet
If our bodies will hold out
    not wear down to aches and pains or worse
we can see this through

    the last long preparations for launch
    of a daughter into the world
But now
    each moment is precious
      if not always easy
    the golden glow before the new day
    another season in our lives
    together, before, during, and after
For change is coming
    But not yet.

Anniversary, November 28, 2008

Twenty-two years, to the day
It seems every so often
Our wandering anniversary
Lands on the twenty-eighth again
Back then, I was the Assistant Professor
With a school year to finish
You were what, a PHS Lieutenant?
Teaching nutrition to new mothers
We lived apart for another six months
Now, twenty-two years later
(such a nondescript number,
not even a designated type of gift)
I'm the Health Communication Specialist
Managing an evaluation software helpdesk
And you're the retired Captain
Team Mom and Craft Queen
And we are the parents
Of an eighteen-year-old high school senior
Living for basketball and college applications
Her eyes on a new life in New England
While living through many lasts
Last year of high school, last year at home
Last volleyball match, last basketball game, last track meet
Last prom, last class, last childhood
New driver, new voter, new adult
Eager for the future at some far-off college
So, we ride the wave, up, down, wait, rush
Holding each moment as long as we can
Without spoiling her eagerness to grow
Knowing next year
She will be a voice on the phone
A text message, a holiday guest
Loved, longed for, but far away

And we will be two again, not three
Two, with the third part of our heart elsewhere
And different waves to ride
Up, down, up, down
But together.

Seven Things I Should Have Told My Daughter When Dropping Her off at Smith College

1.   You have a good head on your shoulders. Now is the time to use it. Don't believe everything you are told, whether by professors or other students. Think things through. Remember that common sense is not common, but rare.

2.   Take care of yourself. Look both ways before crossing the street. Get your flu shots. Remember that there are two people down in Georgia that care about you more than you care about yourself.

3.   Remember that actions have consequences. So do inactions. What you do or don't do in college, in class and out, will affect your entire life. Think long term when making hard choices.

4.   You are going to meet many new people and even more new ideas. Give them all a chance, but understand that many of them will not stand up to close examination or the test of time. But some will.

5.   Try to learn from other people, especially other people's mistakes. You will have enough hard lessons as it is; those learned from observation hurt a lot less than those learned from experience.

6.   You are in college to learn. That is the first priority and the true joy of college. But the classroom and library are not the only places to learn. You also learn in your dorm room, in the cafeteria, on the playing field or court, in the student center, in meeting rooms, etc. You are not just studying academic subjects, but also people and life.

7.   Remember what I do for a living. There is very little human that could surprise me. We can talk about anything. But remember that I have my job because too many people made poor choices. Please don't become one of them.
       Now, little bird, while we love you like life itself, it is time for you to learn to fly.

The Cup of Tears

At the last event of the day
the reception on the lawn outside the auditorium
where we were to meet some of the professors
before saying good-bye
they served lemonade in clear plastic cups
with blue napkins
It was the blue napkin
my wife used to dab her eyes
long after the lemonade was gone
trying to keep the tears from flowing
so that mother and daughter both
would not dissolve into tears
as the time for parting neared
Eventually, with the help of two deans
and a dorm president
the daughter was calmed enough
to give out two hugs
and walk slowly into her future
while the parents, mother still catching tears in her napkin
took a longer way back to their car
stopping to examine an old elm tree
so that our paths would not cross
At the car, the mother jammed the damp napkin
into the plastic cup and set it in the cup holder
as we drove away.

The Twenty-Third Year (Anniversary 2009)

The year things changed
The year of lasts and firsts
Last basketball game
Last track meet
Last high school report card
First college admission
First parent orientation
First real good-bye
We are two and a half now
Elizabeth, smart Elizabeth
First-year Smithie
Now more there than here
More college student up north
Than daughter down the hall
We parent by phone, email, and Skype
Proud of the doors she has opened
Proud of where she is going
Aching in the empty space left behind
That is called growing up
So we too have to grow now
Grow into being a couple again
Grow into a new stage of life
Find new ways to be ourselves
Just as hail and floods
Force us into new roofs and walls
Into reshaping our yard and drive
Replacing doors and windows
So time forces us to quilts and fabrics
Art and drawing for you
Back to books and writing
Job and theatre for me
So time is pushing us now
A new wave of life on the horizon

Relearning how to swim
To ride the swells
Keep our heads above the water
To hold on to each other in the ups and downs
Just hold on, hold on
Hold on.

Shuttle Landing

The bird from space
flew over the swamp
touching down on the incongruous concrete
sending the ibis and egrets flying away
only the eagle remained
circling the strange bird
riding the thermals and vented gasses
examining the rare creature
that flew higher than he.

Thank You, Harry Potter

The credits rolled like years
at the end of *Death Hallows 2*
as I sat beside my daughter
a little tear in each eye
Harry had started as a bedtime story
read to a little girl with dyslexia
lying beside her, a few pages a night
to keep the reading dream alive
books, then audiobooks
(Jim Dale as everybody)
then the movies
I read to her
then listened with her
and watched them all beside her
Seven books, eight movies
one youth, shared
She reads the textbooks at Smith now
and is bound for Spain
where she will turn twenty-one in Cordoba
But something ended
when the credits did
that is also a passing milestone
She and Harry Potter
grown and going
and grateful I will remain
for the sharing.

Last Night

Last night at the restaurant
While eating my birthday cobbler
With my wife
The two of us

And our empty nest
A man came in with his daughter
Perhaps ten she was
Proud to be grown up
And eating with her father
The two of them
Sharing a table and time
And I almost cried
Knowing my time
For such moments
Is almost past.

Anniversary, 2010

There is no prescribed present for a twenty-fourth anniversary
No near-silver, almost as precious metal or gem
Did you know that?
It's like we have to make it one more year
To have actually achieved anything
It's like Elizabeth needing to make it one more year
To be really grown up
As if being twenty and a student at Smith isn't quite enough
I disagree
A retired Commissioned Corps Captain going back to college
To become an artist
Sounds like quite a big deal to me
Like a life at the beginning of a chapter
Not an end
We are not waiting till next year
We are living now
(At least as much as one can live while paying college tuition)
We do not wait for a silver tray or a silver watch
We have today
There is no award for making it to today
Today is an award.

The Silver One

Twenty-five years
        a long time
From looking for a job
        to looking toward retirement
From Commissioned Corps junior officer
        to retired Captain, now BFA student
From two to three
        to empty nest
Baby to ballet to basketball
        to Smith to Spain

We get a silver spoon
        Give ourselves plane tickets
To see the young woman
        we used to hold
Before she begins
        her Grand Tour.

Now pictures line the fireplace
        videos fill the shelves
We have a history now
        moments old and new
Memories shared of heatless nights
        gulls hanging in air, bodysurf beaches
        ghost tours, play performances
        hospital beds, long drives through green valleys
        doing things quietly so the kid would not hear
        cats we have known
        houses we have loved
        times that were ours
More than nine thousand days
        when it has not been
        you and me
But we and us.

Barcelona

Walking back from La Rambla
as my age began to show
my daughter took my arm
in the Spanish style
and began
to take care of me.

The First Leaf

The first leaf of fall
fell like an old woman
fragile and bent
lighter and more brittle
than when the sap flowed
through her veins
blown by the breeze
knowing she would not rise again.

Countries Visited by Elizabeth Davis during Her Twenty-First Year of Life

1. USA
2. Spain
3. Portugal
4. Morocco
5. Ireland
6. Northern Ireland
7. Scotland
8. Belgium
9. Germany
10. Poland
11. Czech Republic
12. Austria
13. Switzerland
14. Italy
15. Vatican City
16. Hungary
17. France
18. England
19. Greece
20. Puerto Rico
21. Canada

Poem for Elizabeth

Write a poem for Elizabeth
Your mother said
For Christmas
To show her friends
Tell her how proud we are
      Of her being at Smith
      Traveling in Europe
      Applying to grad school
And those things are true
We are very proud of you
But I am even more impressed
      By how you make friends
      And the kind of friends you make
      By how you handle the hard work
      And the hard times
      By how you have become aware of the world
      And aware of yourself
You are becoming an adult
      A woman of the world
      A person worth knowing
      Someone on the way
And, yes, we are proud
      We are impressed
And we love what you are
      And will be.

Year Twenty-Six (Anniversary 2012)

It was the year we traveled

Christmas in Madrid
    That little hostel on the fourth floor
    Spanish ham and chocolates
    Mass in Spanish, hot chocolate thick as pudding
    Amazed that the stores opened back up so soon
New Year in Granada
    That fancy restaurant on the hill
    Fireworks over the Alhambra
    Streets so small even the taxies had problems
Your trip of a lifetime to Spain
    If you ignore the tour bus group
    That gave me and Elizabeth bronchitis
    But a glimpse of Elizabeth's life in Cordoba
    The squares in Seville and Madrid
    The hunt for manger scene figures
    Cathedrals, mosques, and museums
    Scenes from books, from dreams, made real
And we were together
    A family again
    On holiday in Spain
    Memories shared forever
Then we flew home
And Elizabeth flew off on her Grand Tour
    Twenty-one countries in her twenty-first year
    Europe in winter, eighteen countries
    On her own, alone, in the snow
    Sitting beside survivors in Auschwitz
    Getting antibiotics in Austria
    Home in May, then off to Puerto Rico
    Anthropology in the mountains
    Then history in Cherokee, Georgia

   And we rejoined her for one more country
   Le Quebec, Canada
   Almost two countries all by itself
Then she goes back to Smith
   Her Senior Year
   The last drop of adolescence
   Turning twenty-two, headed out to life
But your senior year too
   BFA in sight
   Nutritionist to officer to crafter to artist
   And off to China you go
   Maymester half a world away
   A different world, Asian, crowded,
   Nothing you had dreamed of
   But a different vision, unexpected
And now we are back home
   We have all come a long way
   And stand two or three steps
   From the next stages of life
   Grad school? Peace Corps?
   Artist? Quilting expert?
   Close to retirement?
We have seen the world
We stand on one edge or another
Sometimes we stand shoulder-to-shoulder
Sometimes we stand miles apart
But one thing we have learned from all this travel
We stand together.

Graduation, Class of 2013

Despite the forecast
The sky had only puffy white shade
All morning
While the speeches were made
And the seven hundred graduates walked across the stage
Only after the luncheon
As the cars were packed
And the seniors drove off
One by one
Into wherever
Did the sky
Gently, quietly
Begin to weep.

Squirrel

The squirrel pauses
atop the stump of the old oak tree
remembering.

Freeze the Wind

I want to freeze the wind
have it hang there in stillness
and wait for me
before moving on.

My Old Cat

When my old cat
curls up on blanket bed
does she dream kitten dreams
of leap and pounce?
When she seeks
a warm lap
for an evening nap
is it age she hopes to soothe
or some vague memory
of a warm litter of sisters?
Do we share in our old age
some dream of what was?

I Don't Remember

I don't remember exactly when
I stopped feeling
When the soaring hawk
Lifted only my eyes
When a touch
Became only a sensation
Not a communication
When I became so close
To coming apart
That nothing could reach me
Without shattering the glass
So I stopped feeling

But I don't remember exactly when.

Twenty Thirteen Anniversary

What a year.
The ups and downs, the highs and lows, yeses and nos
Dual senior projects, final exams, commencements
You one of thousands in the football arena, E one of hundreds on the
    ageless quad
You, BFA added to MPH, art show acceptances and rejections
E, the BA, History and Anthro, then grad school nos
until a first pick long wait through the hot summer yes
Then the hustle to Boston, find an apartment, learn to ride the green line,
assemble the furniture, find the bagel place, another good-bye and
    good luck in school
Off to the Jersey shore, weddings and reunions for you
broken on the ride home by microfractures in my mother's spine
Ninety-five she is in July, no meds, no doctor
Suddenly fainting and falls, spasms and pain, rehabs and nightmares
Then the lump. Not even a choice, really. No tamoxifen and observation.
No, this one is angry, aggressive, threatening to break through
So surgery in October, mastectomy, rehab centers
Finally, no going home for her
Off to assisted living in November
And Donna begins to come apart, retreating into her room,
hiding from what she cannot control

So now we come to Thanksgiving and anniversary and soon
    Christmas
Days of joy and grace and family rejoined
With Mom fading and fragile
Donna pushing boundaries and patience
Elizabeth, now twenty-three, learning why most people don't go to
    grad school,
And hanging in through hard times
And we
We

You rise to the occasion
I do the best I can
We
This is not where we are supposed to be
Compressed like a Cuban sandwich
Between old and young
We
Should be more than just enduring, getting through
But you sometimes want to cry after dealing with my mother
And I am just tired and hurting in my bones
We
Should be more than this
But at least
We are
We.

The Twenty-Eighth, (Anniversary 2014)

It was not a good year
This year leading up to our twenty-eighth
My mother's long dying
All the sad trips to that sad city
Elizabeth working straight through the summer
Internship and classes
No vacation for anyone
The petty politics of quilting bees
My little brush with cancer
And long recovery
No, not a good year
Except
Change is coming
One way or another
Things will change
We hope for the better
Careers, Art Shows, beginnings and endings
Things will change
Except
For one thing
We will deal with change
The way we dealt with this long year
Together.

Anniversary 2015

Twenty-nine
Another prime
At least as numbers go
Not quite one of the big even years that gets so much attention
More a transition
A going from one state of being to another
Elizabeth from student to employee
From dependent to independent
Not even a Georgian anymore for the first time in her life,
But a Tar Heel, making her own way
And David, a CDC employee no more
Retired, for better or worse
For richer or poorer
To a literary life
Kathy, former nutritionist, former PHS Captain,
Now quilter, BFA fabric artist, wife to a husband underfoot
How will we cope?
David and Kathy, twenty-nine years later
Aches, pains, and Medicare
Graying, into the autumn
Turning to each other for warmth
Turning to each other for company
Turning to each other.

Anniversary 2016

Has it been thirty years?
Elizabeth is twenty-six, so it must be.
'86–'96, '96–'06, '06–'16, yeah, I guess so.
10,956 days, if I got the leap years right
(2000 wasn't a leap year).
That's 5/11 of my life, 10/21 of yours.
Not quite the majority, but getting there.
One apartment, two houses, about six cars, three cats
Four parents passing away, one daughter born and raised
Two careers completed, two active retirements begun
Two lives, a couple of disagreements, lots of laughs
The usual tears and regrets, though fewer than expected.
Counting up the years
All those nights and days
In sickness and in health, etc.
Time leaves aches and scars behind
But most of them were worth it
All those vacations; battlefields and college towns, beaches and
      history,
Military motels, Capes, mountain passes, riverwalks, and deserts.
Elizabeth; ballet and basketball, *Harry Potter* and Smith,
Costumes, candy, summer camps, morning drop-offs, and afternoon
      pickups.
Plays written and seen, quilts sewn and given
Two lives, plus one almost on her own.
Not bad, all things considered
Not the big stage, but a good performance
Useful, mostly peaceful,
With at least a little more to go.
Still a little light before the sunset.
Together even when alone
Two lives, divergent, parallel, convergent,
One.

At Rise We See

At rise we see
At rise we see
At rise we see
Or maybe we don't
Conflict
Must have conflict
Inciting incident
Characters with desires
At rise we see
At rise we see
At rise we see
That we don't
That comes at resolution
When the crisis reveals
And the denouement heals
What we don't see
At rise.

Sixty

When I was sixty
I reached out
And held my mother's hand
Crossing the street
Like I was
A little boy again
But this time
I was the guide.

Aunt Dot

At my last aunt's funeral
(ninety-seven, WWII vet, five great-great-grandchildren)
as the procession drove to the cemetery
the on-coming cars, in the old way of small southern towns,
to show respect
pulled to the side of the road and stopped
to let the dead pass by
this made my wife cry.

The West

We went to see the West
Cheyenne, Custer, the Black Hills
(Crazy Horse, one-lane tunnels, buffalo, Rushmore)
Rapid City, Badlands (Indian fry bread, big horn sheep, sun moving on rocks, lots of sky)
Sturgis, Deadwood (souvenir shops both)
Across empty, magnificent, high Wyoming
Cody (museum, rodeo, high dam)
Yellowstone (rapids, mud pots, geysers, falls, cliffs, passes, valleys, ospreys, marmots, buffalo, buffalo, buffalo)
Beartooth Pass into alpine ice in August (elevation nearly eleven thousand feet, clouds at nine thousand)
Down to Red Lodge for quiet and quilting
Then bisecting Wyoming north to south in one day
To catch the metal bird from Denver to home
Scenery, history, tales, and lore, all as wondrous as the pictures in the brochure
Sights almost as spectacular as the photos in the tourist books
It was as advertised, and advertised, and advertised
Ah yes, I recognize that. I saw the National Geographic Special
Yes, the guidebook was right, that is interesting
But all a bit too familiar
To actually inspire a poem.

Anniversary 2017, the Thirty-First

It was a year of places
this year after thirty years
now thirty-one and counting
we went and went and went
to the Georgia Athens for Joanna's wedding
and months later to little Union Point
to see her new house and eat her chef's cooking
as irony of irony, she can't for now
then wandering Long Island in the snow from Sound to shore
Michael's wedding this time
visiting Wengens old and new
who behaved like we were family
your brother bought you beer from Poughkeepsie
Amanda breastfed Alexander after feeding us sandwiches
Michael planned his honeymoon the day after the wedding
    as we sat in the living room before leaving
    with good memories and a picture of all the Wengens together
in spring to Wrightsville Beach and Wilmington
for a long weekend with Elizabeth
beaches and battleships, gardens and trolley horses pissing in the
    streets
warm enough for ice cream but not quite for swimming
(Of course, Elizabeth had her own adventure later with Joanna
off to Harry Potter World, the almost-magic one in Orlando,
childhood's magic touching her once again)
Then the big anniversary/birthday/Christmas present trip out West
quilting conference exploding into expedition
flying into Denver (which I don't think we ever actually saw)
after passing over squares and irrigation circles in Kansas
that reminded Kathy of a quilt she had yet to make
north to Cheyenne for the night where the traffic finally thinned out

then off to the Black Hills (where cell phone service died for the rest of
> the trip, leaving only Skype and emails for touching base with
> Elizabeth, and sometimes not even that)

impressive, gigantic, incomplete Crazy Horse (and the Native
> American displays)

unimpressive, crowded, overexposed Rushmore (perhaps, for us, too
> much like Stone Mountain)

bison, donkeys, and deer, the rocks and crags

penetrated by needle-thin serpentine asphalt

two-way tunnels wide enough for one car

switch-backs and pigs-tails

five-mile-per-hour speed limits that nobody broke

Rapid City, land of presidential statues, a base to explore

Sturgis on a Sunday morning, before the motorcycles arrived but full
> of noisy T-shirts

Deadwood, one-road tourist town, living off the memory of silver and
> shootouts

From Lead to Spearfish, the beautiful river valley, fishermen and
> waders

getting in some afternoon summer sun before the leaves turn colors in
> late August

then a quick stop at Wall Drug in Wall
> for free ice water and Kathy's veteran's free coffee and donut
> plus lots of non-free souvenirs

on to the Badlands, erosion gone wild, geologic glory, and big-horn
> sheep
> > earth-tones turned bold, light color-shifting the stark world
> > the Sioux-run motel that doled out ice from a bag
> > tiny interior, just outside the park, with wild turkeys in the
> > street

outside the one store

then the long drive, back through empty Wyoming, mountains and
> plains

populated mostly by cattle and quilt shops

snow fences and treeless scenery

to Cody, the artificial town Buffalo Bill created
      rodeo and gunfights every night
      five grand museums
(Western art, guns, Indians, animals, and Buffalo Bill each get one)
plus statues, graves, dams, and a real Western town
a fitting preparation for Yellowstone
The Park, geysers and hot springs coming in colors,
steam seeping from the ground, imitating mist
waterfalls and wildness, rapids and canyons
a volcano caldera asleep, for now, letting us see it breathe and snore
two days based at Old Faithful, exploring hot pools and mud pots
three days at the Canyon of the Yellowstone
      Upper and Lower Falls, among other falls and rapids
      plus buffalo, a deer, birds, and multiple rodents
      (but no bear, moose, or wolves)
all very beautiful, impressive, wondrous, etc.
but strangely familiar for something not seen before, unsurprising
too much remembered from National Geographic, TV travel specials,
      and nature films
yes, I have seen this before, in pictures at least
more like meeting a TV star from a long-running series and hundreds
      of talk shows
yes, I know you though we have never met before
then the high point of the trip, at least literally
over the Beartooth Pass, almost ten thousand feet up
      arctic tundra, iced-up mountain-sides in August
      mountain scenery that went on forever
      until the clouds came down to road level
      (thank you Toyota 4Runner)
      missing part of the views
      but earning Kathy a T-shirt
then lodging in Red Lodge
though up to Billings for one day
to set a record of six quilt shops shopped between sunrise and sunset
you to the quilting classes

me reading and recovering
nothing as quiet as a ski lodge in August
        hummingbird moths attacking flowers
        rocky creeks doing background burbles
        staff from Turkey, of all places
finally the long drive down I-25
seeing actual towns in Wyoming
picking the same restaurant in Casper
        as two other wandering quilters
finding a motel in Loveland, Colorado,
        back in the traffic
a few more souvenirs the next morning
then off to the airport, back over Kansas
to the end of yet another trip of a lifetime
Of course, this doesn't count the trips to Salisbury to see Elizabeth
        (or the stops in Spartanburg to see Donna)
the long and occasionally longer weekends
        trying to sample every restaurant in Salisbury and vicinity
        especially the barbeque joints,
        and hit the high points of every town in driving distance
        from Charlotte up to Greensboro
        historic sights and museums, downtowns and local food
seeing Elizabeth in her new life and times
        touching holidays and memories while we can
And so, the year has passed from place to place, place by place
in the process, Kathy has lost more weight and made more quilts
I compiled all my old poems in case anybody ever wants to read them
        by going through too many boxes, files, and notebooks
        and wrote some other stuff and lots of agent queries
we went, we stayed, we were
soon we will both be on Medicare
        and officially old
we take walks in the parks
        and hope it helps

we have a few more scars, a couple more specialists on the medical
    provider list
I'm missing a little slice of my tongue
Kathy will soon be out a tooth
we both now have joints that complain about the years
    though I think mine still outnumber hers
but Kathy has quilts in process and plans for more
I think I have at least one more book in me, agent or not
we keep going, more slowly, with another pain or two
    getting on each other's nerves sometimes
    but that passes
we travel well together
going to other places near or far or here
Elizabeth has her own adventures to follow
    though we do that from more and more afar
    Godspeed her where she may go
we have our own road to go, short or long
so, we keep going, together
knowing, after all this time
it's the only way to go.

Sunset

Geese flying into the sunset
Say my own sun is setting
I do not fear being dead
I do fear dying
If there is a God anywhere close to good
He owes me one
If not, I do not fear being nothing
But from is to was sounds painful
Change never comes easy
So I do not fear the night
I fear the fading of the light.

Pain

Pain can be your friend
        For about five seconds
Warning you something is wrong
        So you can fix it.
After that, pain is just pain
        In the neck, in the butt, wherever
An alarm that will not turn off
        A siren that will not be silenced.
Constant, recurring, intractable
        All types of aches that become the problem
Something to endure, live with, cope with
        Even die from, in time.
Life becomes unbearable, a pain
        On a scale of one to ten
Do two threes and a five make an eleven?
        Do neck spasms, degenerated discs
And a worn-out knee add up
        Or multiply?

Anniversary 2018

We are both officially old now
With Medicare cards to prove it
Signing up for Social Security
And getting the Senior Special at Sweet Tomato
    Without having to ask

I guess that's to be expected
After all, Harry Truman was still president when I was born
And Ike in his first year in office for you
Figures out of history books for most people today
    Fading into myths

So we have both made it to old
Baby Boomers past our boom
Walking slowly into our Golden Years
Not sure how much is gold
    And how much gilt

Hoping for a few more sunrises
Scenic views and overlooks
Touches of tomorrow to feel
Like something of us will go on
    Even if we aren't here

Elizabeth has moved closer
Living in Decatur and working for the state
Sometimes splitting costs with us on trips
And coming over to help with heavy chores
    Another change in who takes care of whom

And we are to the point where change is probably not a good thing
Retirement is no longer a novelty
We both ache in one body part or another
Our doctors say we are simply wearing out
    And only some parts are repairable

Growing old is not for sissies they say

    Not for the faint of heart
    Those lacking grit
But maybe I can handle it
    If you are here
    Warming me
Reminding me of what was
    And is
    Between us
Uniting us
    As the light fades
    And the cold seeps in.

Random Lines

I have so many pens
So few words.

My cat moves to follow the sun
Across the room
Until it is gone.

Even spring can get old
When what you want
Is heat.

Spring

Ah, the sounds of spring
The buzz of the lawnmowers
The twitter of the string trimmers
The chirps of the leaf blowers

Yes, spring, when the world comes back to life
As daylight savings time commands the sun to shine longer
And April showers bring lightning strikes
And towns test their tornado sirens

Spring, when pollen bursts forth into sneezes
Coloring our cars a dull yellow
Making us all forget
How bad winter really was.

2020

It was the year we stayed in.
COVID, COVID, COVID.
It started well.
Going to the Shakespeare Tavern for Twelfth Night on Twelfth Night
David's ten-minute play done at Oglethorpe days later
Elizabeth visited for Kathy's birthday celebration.
Then everything got canceled.
No playwright's group, no quilt retreat, no Braves games, no Renaissance Festival,
No summer vacation, no trips to see Donna, no church breakfasts, no maids cleaning.
Self-quarantine it was called
Basic self-defense against mindless virus and unmasked idiots
Bad things rippled outward
Elizabeth's job, and hundreds of others, was abolished to salvage the state budget

Thousands of other people, millions, ended up on unemployment
Wise beyond her years, Elizabeth had already moved apartments and canceled cable
To reduce expenses and be ready for whatever
And it came and went and came and went and came back again, stronger, crueler
Some events survived, mostly on *Zoom*.
David's novel, *The Mistakes*, was published
But hardly promoted in the middle of a pandemic
Kathy had artwork in a show at the Alpharetta Art Center
That almost nobody went to, including Kathy
Elizabeth eventually got another job with the state
Setting up data collection for mental hospitals
Joe Biden got elected, ending part of the nightmare, we hope
Getting somebody who will at least try to save lives
But mostly it was just you and me
Here in the house
Touching others only by phone or social media
So we touched each other
And held on tight
And remembered why we can live with each other
Why we can love each other
Through anything
Even having only each other to lean on
In the year of the COVID.

Spring

After seventy springs
> some of the wonder is gone

Yes, the azaleas are glorious this year
> the blazing reds, burning pinks, pure whites

As are the blushing cherry blossoms
> and brief Chinese magnolias

Life turning green again
> Earth reborn, yada, yada, yada

As it has every year for millions of springs
> and will for millions more

If we don't screw it up too bad
> which we darn well might

I guess that is the wonder after all
> that Mother Nature persists

Despite us
> and makes each leaf and petal

A resistance fighter
> against ignorance and stupidity.

Anniversary 2021

And another year of COVID survived
Death racing to claim the victims of ill luck, ignorance, or illogic
We surviving on insolation, masks, and vaccines
All three of us among the first in line for shots in January
Life lived in small doses, virtually when possible

But not a year of nothing
Elizabeth got her second shot the day she left state employ
And became a CDC Fed, for at least thirteen months
Pushing the vaccine and other vaccinations for adults

Kathy had her cataracts removed

Replaced by reading glasses scattered all over the house
David had a Zoom reading of his Angel, which flew away
Not yet heard from again
A new cat moved in and proved a very different cat
A lap cat full of bad habits and demands

Elizabeth risked the virus gods to visit her friends on the West Coast
The physicist and the research librarian
Riding trains over the mountains, walking the wet streets
Getting back just before the bomb cyclones started exploding offshore

And we are about to have our lives torn apart and renovated,
At least the master bathroom and bedroom parts
Maybe, if the supplies come in and workers appear,
Disrupting the end and beginning of the years

No, not a year without events
Just a year lived as internally as possible
Drawing on each other for company, for society, for love
Finding our survival in each other
Making the best of our ailing world.

December 2021

The inflatable Christmas decorations
(Frostys, Santas, elves, and reindeer)
lie prostrate across the lawn
powerless to rise
like survivors of a drunken orgy
on Sunday morning
Capturing, perhaps better than their upright selves
the deflated spirit
of a covid Christmas.

Arising

The bed squeaks
The floor creaks
My joints crack
A symphony of age.

Marcie

In the dark night
Listening to "a once-in-a-generation cold front" blow in
I think of the card your sister sent
Giving your end date
And I shiver.

About the Author

David Davis wrote a science fiction novel entitled *The Mistakes*, published by Kohler Books in 2020. In 2023, he also published a collection of essays on science and religion, *Seven Heretical Sermons*, and a collection of detective short stories, *The Detectives*. Some of the poems in this collection were previously published in his book, *Heartspan*. In addition, he has had seventeen plays produced, including productions in New York and Hollywood. Many of these plays will be published in his forthcoming book, *Selected Plays*. He has also had several poems, magazine features, and scholarly articles published. He earned a PhD in theatre and is a member of the Dramatists Guild and Working Title Playwrights. He has worked as a physics and math teacher, actor, head of three college theatre programs, technical writer, editor, and health communications specialist. He currently lives in Atlanta, Georgia, with his wife, Kathy, and has one daughter, Elizabeth.

Other Books by David Davis

The Mistakes

Seven Heretical Sermons

The Detectives

Heartspan